# ST. LOUIS UNION STATION
# AND ITS RAILROADS

ST. LOUIS
UNION STATION

*Norbury L. Wayman*

# AND ITS RAILROADS

*To my favorite ladies,*
*St. Louis Union Station*
*and my wife, Amy.*

©1987 by Norbury L. Wayman
ISBN 0-9616356-1-4
Library of Congress No. 86-217654

Published by The Evelyn E. Newman Group,
St. Louis, Missouri

Cover photograph by Denny Silverstein

Graphic design by Susan Wooleyhan
and Shelley Dieterichs

**Frontispiece:** The Grand Hall of
Union Station, c. 1985

# ACKNOWLEDGMENTS

I would like to express my grateful appreciation for the valuable assistance and information from these individuals and organizations in the preparation of this book.

Association of American Railroads
John W. Barriger III Railroad Library—Mercantile Library Association of St. Louis
Mark J. Cedeck—National Railway Historical Society
Gulf, Mobile & Ohio Historical Society
Walter A. Fussner—Missouri Pacific Railroad—Union Pacific System
Hellmuth, Obata & Kassabaum, Inc.—Architects
Patrick D. Hiatte—Burlington Northern Railroad
Missouri Historical Society
National Museum of Transport, St. Louis
Eric P. Newman, St. Louis
Omni International Hotels
Oppenheimer Properties, Inc.
The Pullman Company
The Rouse Company
St. Louis Community Development Agency
St. Louis Public Library
St. Louis Regional Commerce and Growth Association
Donald A. Sarno, St. Louis
Terminal Railroad Association of St. Louis

All illustrations are from the author's collection unless otherwise noted.

*Norbury L. Wayman*
*St. Louis, Missouri—1987*

Ruth A. Shoults

**Telegrapher Ivy W. Allen and a friend, both employees of the Frisco Railway in 1919, ham it up on a facsimile of one of its famous trains.**

# CONTENTS

The port cochere, Union Station's elegant coach entrance, was sacrificed to progress when Market Street was widened in 1911 to accommodate the new-fangled horseless carriages.

# INTRODUCTION

It was inevitable that St. Louis, due to its central geographical location, would become a major U.S. transportation center. But because the city relied upon river traffic as its earliest means of connection with the hinterlands and with other inland marine ports, its debut as an important railroad center was delayed until after the Civil War.

The war and its attendant difficulties for a commercial and industrial city in a border state caused St. Louis to lag behind Chicago in economic growth and railroad development. While steamboat commerce on the rivers was responsible for the spectacular rise of St. Louis in antebellum years, the Mississippi River was also a formidable barrier to its accessibility by railroads. This situation was finally relieved with the opening of Eads Bridge at St. Louis in 1874, but the river had by then been bridged for 18 years at Rock Island, Illinois, which allowed widespread construction of railroads from Chicago into the northwestern Mississippi Valley.

Despite these historical disadvantages, St. Louis was not to be denied distinction as a rail center. Before 1900, the city firmly claimed its niche as the nation's second most important railroad hub. Union Station was a major element in that attainment.

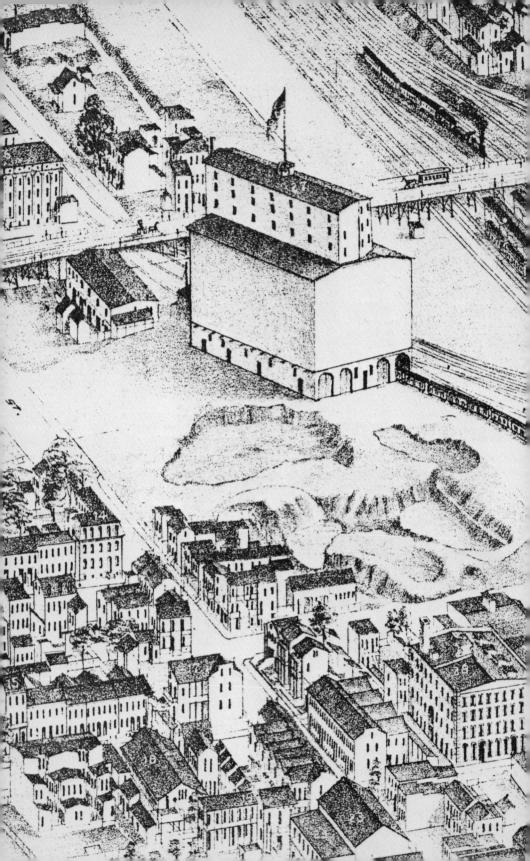

# PART I

*St. Louis Railroad Passenger Depots and the Evolution of Union Station*

The old Union Depot at Twelfth and Poplar (building with smokestack) was the modest forerunner of St. Louis Union Station. Railroad traffic outgrew it within ten years.

Newman Collection

**Created by a miller who dammed a stream in the 1760s, Chouteau's Pond became a gathering place long before a train station was built on part of the site. Although the pond was drained in 1850, the area is still known as Mill Creek Valley.**

B y a chronological skein of reasoning, the history of Union Station's site can be traced back to the days of colonial St. Louis. When St. Louis was founded by Pierre Laclede Liguest in 1764, a small stream, named by the French La Petite Riviere, flowed into the Mississippi a short distance south of the village. Among the first settlers was Joseph Taillon, a miller from Cahokia, a settlement on the east bank of the river, who expressed interest in establishing a mill in St. Louis. Consequently, Laclede granted Taillon a tract of about a thousand acres on both sides of the stream westward to its source near present-day Vandeventer Avenue. (Its other boundaries were from the present Market Street to Chouteau Avenue, and east to Fourth Street.) Taillon, phonetically spelled as Tayon, was the original name of Eighteenth Street, which borders Union Station on the east.

Taillon built his log mill near what is now the intersection of Eighth and Spruce streets and dammed the stream to form a mill pond. Three years later Taillon gave up the operation, conveying the mill and its tract to Laclede, who operated it until his death in 1779. The tract was then sold at auction to Auguste Chouteau for two thousand livres, payable in shaved deerskins, a value of about 50 cents an acre. Chouteau rebuilt the mill with stone and raised the height of the dam, greatly increasing the area of Chouteau's mill pond. The mill proved successful, and Chouteau continued to operate it until his death in 1829, after which the tract was divided among his heirs.

Meanwhile, the pond had become a recreational attraction for the inhabitants of St. Louis, a trysting place for lovers, and a popular spot for housewives to do their laundry. In addition to rain water runoff, the pond was fed by several springs, including Rock Spring at the creek's source and some others along the edges of the pond. As St. Louis grew, Chouteau's Pond became rimmed with industries such as Collier's Lead Works, breweries, and (at its western end) dairy farms.

During the 1830s and 1840s, epidemics of cholera were frequent in St. Louis. Medical authorities pointed an accusing finger at the polluted waters of Chouteau's Pond as a source of the disease. After the great cholera epidemic of the summer of 1849, when thousands died and many fled the city, it was decreed that the pond be drained. Despite strenuous protests by the Chouteaus, the pond became extinct in 1850-51.

However, the drainage ultimately proved beneficial to the city, because it provided a start for a modern sewer system: the Mill Creek trunk sewer was built along the bed of the old Petite Riviere.

A second benefit soon became apparent with the arrival of railroads on the St. Louis scene. The low level and easy grades of the creek valley gave it an excellent alignment into the heart of the city from the west. Mill Creek Valley became the obvious site for railroad yards of the future.

The first of the railroads to take advantage of this newly developed windfall was the Pacific, forerunner of the Missouri Pacific Railroad. Its first station was a wooden shed, built in 1852, on the west side of Fourteenth Street near Poplar in Mill Creek Valley. This was the first railroad depot in St. Louis at a time when the Pacific Railroad extended only as far west as Kirkwood. As the railroad was built farther westward and more business developed, a more central depot became necessary. This need was met with a more ambitious wooden structure on the west side of Seventh Street at Poplar in 1854. This was the Pacific Railroad's principal passenger and freight station until the completion of the first Union Depot 20 years later. It was then demolished, and the site became the location of the Missouri Pacific's freight department.

Soon after the opening of the Pacific Railroad, two other railroads entered St. Louis along the riverfront from opposite directions. From the south came the St. Louis & Iron Mountain Railroad, which built a two-room wooden station at Main and Plum streets. At about the same time, a similar wooden depot was erected for the North Missouri Railroad (later the Wabash) at Second and North Market streets.

With improvements in the railroad business, the Iron Mountain later constructed a larger depot at Fourth and Plum streets, while the North Missouri station was replaced by a larger Wabash station along the levee. The Ohio & Mississippi Railroad reached Illinoistown (now East St. Louis, Illinois) in 1857.

The decade following the Civil War was a period of remarkable expansion in the nation's railroad system. It became obvious with the completion of Eads Bridge, uniting East and the West through the St. Louis gateway, that a union passenger depot would be necessary to handle the increased traffic. The depot became a major feature of the plan for the bridge and its tunnel, which was to lead trains into the Mill Creek yards at Eighth and Spruce streets.

An earlier plan for this union depot, made in 1870, called for a structure fronting on Washington Avenue between Broadway and Eighth Street. The idea was to excavate the entire area of three blocks, including the streets, down to the level of the tunnel tracks, and then to erect a combination depot, hotel, and office building. However, the project, which would have been impracticable because of the emission of locomotive smoke, failed because of opposition from private interests.

# EADS BRIDGE

It had become apparent early in the nineteenth century that a bridge across the Mississippi River at St. Louis was not only desirable, but essential. An 1839 proposal by Charles Ellet, Jr., builder of America's first suspension bridge, to erect a three-span bridge here failed to muster sufficient civic and financial support. Several other proposals for a bridge were made in the years before the Civil War, with similar results. Most of the opposition to a bridge was generated by the ferry interests, principally the Wiggins Ferry Company, which had a virtual monopoly on river crossings at St. Louis. Some additional antipathy was generated by steamboat owners, who foresaw the bridge as an obstacle to their high smokestacks and the bridge piers as navigational hazards.

Finally, the Illinois and St. Louis Bridge Company was organized and Captain James Buchanan Eads was chosen chief engineer for the

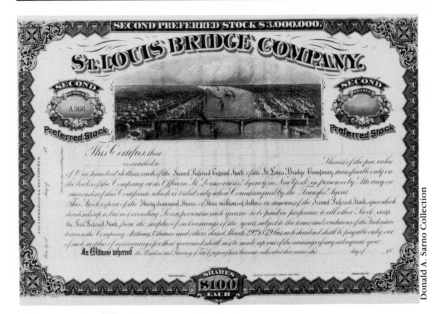

**Shrewd stockholders who wanted a piece of the local action in 1867 invested in the St. Louis Bridge Company, builder of the first span across the Mississippi River at St. Louis.**

project. Even after construction was begun on the bridge in 1867, many St. Louisans ridiculed the idea as being visionary and impossible.

The construction period was plagued by physical handicaps as well as continued litigation. Besides the river's width and powerful currents, the greatest problem was the thickness of sand in the river bed on the east side. Eads ingeniously devised the use of cofferdams and compressed air to hold back leakage while excavating and building the pier foundations. His previous experience in the salvage of sunken steamboats aided in the removal of submerged wrecks.

While the bridge was still being built, the ferry operators succeeded in having it condemned as a navigational hazard through their influence with the Secretary of War. However, Eads and Dr. William Taussig, the bridge company chairman, went to Washington to intercede with President Grant. When Grant learned that the bridge project had been approved by the federal government, the order of condemnation was rescinded. A final natural catastrophe was the tornado of 1871, which played havoc with the construction equipment. In 1874, seven years after its inception, the graceful three-arch span, with its highway and railroad decks, was completed.

Another great engineering achievement built at the same time was a double-track railroad tunnel between the bridge and the railroad yards in Mill Creek Valley. This was created to eliminate the need for running trains through the city streets.

The area of Washington Avenue from Third to Eighth streets and Eighth south to Spruce was excavated to tunnel grade, and massive masonry walls and arches were built to shelter the tracks. (In later years, the mile-long open cut was filled in and paved over; the tunnel's great arches became supports for the streets above.)

On July 4, 1874, the bridge, named for its builder, and the tunnel were dedicated in impressive ceremonies amid parades, elaborate street decorations, and a triumphal arch in honor of the occasion. Now that Eads Bridge was ready for railroad traffic and the bridge company had a contract with eastern railroads for that purpose, it was assumed that they would run their trains across the bridge. However, this did not come about; the railroads alleged that their Illinois charters gave them no right to operate trains in Missouri, and the bridge company had no authority to run a railroad in either state. This problem was not resolved until a year later, when auxiliary railroad companies were organized in Missouri and Illinois to handle freight traffic across the bridge. But there was still no provision for passenger trains.

Newman Collection

**"You can't get there from here"** was the complaint about cross-river train transportation until Eads Bridge (in background), an engineering marvel, was dedicated in 1874. The view is north along Wharf Street.

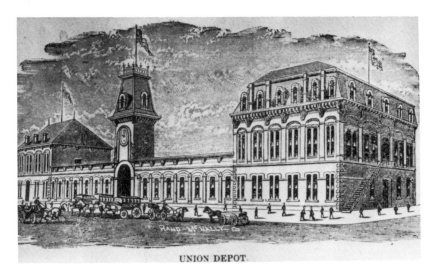

UNION DEPOT.

**The old Union Depot, predecessor of Union Station, was located at Twelfth and Poplar streets in 1875.**

# THE OLD UNION DEPOT

An act of the Missouri legislature on March 18, 1871, had authorized the formation of union depots and stations for railroads in Missouri cities. Under that act, the St. Louis Union Depot Company was formed on May 9, 1874, to erect a depot on the south side of Poplar Street between Ninth and Twelfth streets. This site was chosen after a two-year study.

Plans called for a three-story brick and stone building containing railroad offices on its upper floors and a much larger first floor at track level, including waiting rooms, ticket offices, and other accommodations for the traveling public, all in one location. The depot had 11 tracks, with open shelters covering the platforms between the tracks. An overhead passageway enabled travelers to reach the outlying platforms. This unification of all railroad operations represented a vast improvement over conditions during the pre-bridge years. In those days, passengers on eastern railroads reached St. Louis by ferry and purchased return tickets at the old Planters Hotel. They then reached the ferries by riding omnibuses and having their baggage shipped by transfer companies. On June 13, 1875, a year after the bridge opened, the first passenger train came across it and through the tunnel to discharge its passengers at the new Union Depot.

While the Union Depot was a successful operation during its first few years, despite many defects in its arrangement, eventually the burgeoning passenger traffic outgrew its accommodations. About ten years after its opening, a much larger station was needed for the rapidly growing city of St. Louis.

# THE UNION STATION

Underlying the move for a greater union station was the organization of the Terminal Railroad Association of St. Louis in October 1889. This new group absorbed the terminal railroads on both sides of the river and superseded the Union Depot Company. Six railroads became members of the Terminal Railroad Association: the Ohio & Mississippi (later the Baltimore & Ohio), the Big Four, Louisville & Nashville, Missouri Pacific, Iron Mountain, and Wabash. Eight more lines joined the T.R.R.A. in 1902, followed by the Cotton Belt in 1910. Dr. Taussig was elected president of the association, a position he held until 1896. At a meeting early in 1890, the Terminal Railroad Association decided that the old Union Depot had become inadequate and began planning for a new and considerably larger union station. It would completely consolidate all passenger traffic under one roof.

The first consideration was the choice of a site. This choice was governed by the topographical conditions, which confined railroad approaches within a relatively narrow valley and made the operation of numerous trains difficult and dangerous. This precluded a "through station" embodying the use of many east-west tracks and platforms. It was therefore decided on April 1, 1890, to construct an "end station" plan with north-south stub end tracks entering a vast trainshed. As a result of this track design, no train was able to pass through St. Louis; Union Station was literally a complete terminal.

The chosen site, southwest of Eighteenth and Market streets, was deemed to be the closest area to the downtown district that could accommodate a union station of the great magnitude that was visualized. This site, which extended from Eighteenth to Twentieth streets and from Market Street southward to the southern edge of the railroad yards, included a wide variety of structures. There were more than a hundred houses and several large industrial establishments, including the Uhrig Brewery, a gas plant, a flour mill, a wagon factory, a soap company, warehouses, and the stables of a city streetcar line.

A national architectural competition with a first prize of $10,000 was announced in March 1891. In July, eight sets of plans were received from nationally known architectural firms. The winning design was submitted by the firm of Link and Cameron of St. Louis, whose principal partner, Theodore C. Link, was placed in charge of the project. His design, with some modifications, resulted in Union Station's completed appearance. Differences from the original design in the main facade are explained by the fact that although the plan called for a building with a length of 455 feet, during construction additional property fronting another 150 feet to the west was acquired, requiring an extension of the facade.

St. Louis Public Library

**Railroad stations, unlike airports, strived for local character. Theodore Link's design for Union Station was intended to herald the grandeur of the city.**

Architecturally, a free treatment of the Romanesque style was selected as being well suited to express historically the character and use of the structure. Because a railway station served as a portal to a city, as did bastioned gates in medieval towns, it was interpreted as a modern version of a feudal gateway. Union Station is said to have been inspired by the walled city of Carcasonne in southern France.

In February 1892 the necessary construction permits were obtained from the city, and in April the demolition of buildings and

Anheuser-Busch

**Market Street, circa 1890s: a delivery wagon pauses across from Union Station. The neighborhood was lively one, full of taverns, honky-tonks, pawnshops, tobacconists and other services for rail-weary travelers.**

St. Louis Public Library

All railroads led to the World's Fair as the country began to sing "Meet me in St. Louis, Louis" in 1904. The *World's Fair Bulletin* pictured Union Station as the local hub of activity.

St. Louis Globe-Democrat

"A small circle of friends" attended Union Station's opening night festivities on September 1, 1894. The Grand Hall, shown here, has now been restored to its original glory. (The chandelier, however, fell victim to a scrap metal drive during World War II.)

excavation work was begun. Because the site embraced part of the bed of the old Chouteau's Pond, difficulty was experienced in building heavy foundation walls. Old brewery vaults had to be blown up to make room for walls and piers. Many of the piers under the steel columns supporting the trainshed roof required pile foundations. Foundation work took more than a year, and finally on July 8, 1893, the cornerstone was laid.

Fourteen months later, on September 1, 1894, the great building was ready for public use. It was officially dedicated and opened with an impressive ceremony in Union Station's Grand Hall. The first train to enter Union Station was a fast mail on the Vandalia line, which arrived at 1:45 a.m. on September 2. The principal components of Union Station were the main building or "Headhouse," the Midway (for access to trains), the trainshed (with baggage and mail facilities), express buildings, and a power plant.

Fronting 606 feet along the south side of Market Street west from Eighteenth, the main facade of the Headhouse is Union Station's foremost architectural feature. Its highest point is the east pavilion and the 230-foot clock tower with its four-faced clock, whose dials are ten feet in diameter. The tower was originally intended to house railroad records and to serve as an air shaft to ventilate the Station. It also holds a water tank for the Station's sprinkler system. The tower's stone work, which is rough-hewn at its base, is smooth-finished in the upper portions. Like the rest of the front and sides of the building, the tower was constructed of Bedford (Indiana) limestone. Rear walls of the Headhouse were of gray brick above and buff Roman brick below the roof of the trainshed. Originally, the building's roofs were covered with gray Spanish tiles; they were replaced with the present red tiles in 1949.

The central pavilion, containing the Station's main entrance, is flanked by twin turrets and was originally graced by a porte cochere, which was removed in 1911 when Market Street was widened. To the west, a long section with four stylish dormers terminates in the great gabled Terminal Hotel.

Although the hotel structure was built at the same time as the Station, its interior was not completed until some years later. It had almost a hundred rooms and was administered on the European plan. The hotel served as a stopover for travelers awaiting next-day connections and for railroad crews. Its lobby could be entered from Market Street as well as from the Station's Midway. Above the lobby was an atrium arising for five floors.

The major element in the interior of the Headhouse, which had a depth of 80 feet from the street, was the Grand Hall on the second floor. It was an awe-inspiring sight, with 8,500 square feet of floor space and a barrel-vault ceiling 65 feet high. Originally it was to have been a waiting space for travelers with long layovers between trains, and it contained writing desks and lounge chairs. It was approached from Market Street by a grand staircase with an allegorical mosaic-glass window under its golden entrance arch. This window depicts three great rail terminals of the United States: New York, St. Louis, and San Francisco. Its central female figure, representing St. Louis, is shown seated before the Old Courthouse. Above the window and over the entrance foyer is a "whispering arch," where a person facing the arch on one side can distinctly hear a whisper from someone facing the arch's other side.

High on the arches at each end of the Grand Hall or Grand Waiting Room are seven maidens in plaster relief, with outstretched hands holding light globes. An original accoutrement hanging from the center of the great arched ceiling was an ornate iron chandelier, 20 feet in diameter, holding 350 lights and weighing 4,500 pounds. (During World War II this chandelier fell victim to the wartime scrap metal drive.) Around the Grand Hall's upper levels were arcaded galleries. In the effulgent style of the 1890s, the second floor was elaborately decorated, but the magnificent Grand Hall was the "pièce de résistance" of the entire ensemble. The Grand Hall was flanked originally by a ladies' waiting room on the east, and by a gentlemen's smoking room on the west. Between the latter and the Market Street wall was a passageway called the Gothic Corridor, which led to the Main Dining Hall and private dining rooms. Beneath the Grand Hall and connected to it by the Grand Staircase was the ground floor general waiting room at track level. On its east side were ticket offices, and beyond them a barber shop and a second waiting room.

In the room's center, opposite the main entrance stairway, was the information bureau, while on the waiting room's west side were stores and a post office with a lunch room beyond. Between that and the lobby of the Terminal Hotel was the carriage concourse, used in later years for taxicabs. Upper floors of the Headhouse were occupied by offices of the Terminal Railroad Association and those of various railroads.

Between the Headhouse and the trainshed was a long area about 70 feet wide extending the full length of the Station. This was the Midway, where great throngs of travelers and friends met for greetings or farewells. Here were benches for those eagerly waiting for trains to arrive or depart. At its center on the trainshed side was the great bulletin board, where the track numbers and arrival and departure times of all

**The Midway hummed with activity from the turn of the century through the 1940s. Many people spurned the inside waiting rooms to join its happy hubbub.**

Western Union was the grand old man of communication when Ma Bell was just a girl. Here, telegraphers man their posts in 1895.

The vast trainshed, shown here under construction in 1894, was the brainchild of engineer George H. Pegram. The restored Union Station still uses the skylights he designed.

trains were posted. Behind it was the Stationmaster's office, where the train data were received by "teleautograph" from the control tower in the yards. The Midway gave access from the streets at each end, with a stairway descending into it from Eighteenth Street. The side of the Midway toward Market Street was lined with newstands, locker rooms, and a Fred Harvey restaurant. Harvey opened his first restaurant in St. Louis before the Civil War, in the days when travelers ate hurriedly at station lunch rooms on short stopovers between trains. The Harvey restaurant in Union Station was opened in 1896 and was one of the last Station facilities to close in June 1970.

The Midway was originally covered by a light steel trussed roof of corrugated glass and iron. On the side toward the trainshed, it was separated from direct access to trains by a highly ornamental wrought-iron fence pierced by 16 gates for entry to the train platforms. In later years this fence was replaced by a combination glass and metal frame wall reaching to the ceiling of the Midway. The long crosswise aisle at the end of the tracks was called the "Avenue of the Bumpers." There a bumper control device prevented trains from over-running this transverse space at the end of each track.

At the time of its construction, Union Station's trainshed was the largest in existence and covered more tracks than any other in the world. Trains of 22 railroad companies could be accommodated on its 30 tracks. The main trainshed was 630 feet long and 606 feet wide, covering an area of nearly ten acres. This vast shed, designed by George H. Pegram, was covered by a roof composed of five separate spans. The central one was 141 feet three inches in width, the two intermediate spans were each 139 feet two inches wide and the two outer ones each spanned a width of 90 feet eight inches. In the center of the shed roof throughout its entire length, additional light was provided by a skylight 36 feet wide, covered with heavy corrugated glass supported by copper bars. On its open sides, this skylight provided ample ventilation for the shed. At its outer sides, the shed was supported by steel columns spaced 30 feet apart. These columns, which furnished anchorage for the entire shed, took care of all wind stresses. Inside, the roof was supported by a series of columns, with trusses connecting the columns to the roof. Erection of steel work began on July 7, 1892, and the completed trainshed was ready for occupancy on November 25, 1893.

The Headhouse, Midway, and trainshed occupied 11.1 acres, and when accessory areas were added, the Station itself, exclusive of main track approaches, occupied more than 22 acres. There were 19 miles of track in the Station system, of which 3½ miles were under the shed. The entire outlay for real estate and improvements was nearly $6.5 million, with the Headhouse costing $850,000. This represented a huge amount of money for a single project at that time.

Quite a few changes have occurred in connection with auxiliary buildings in the rail yards south of the trainshed. In 1894, when Union Station was opened, its power plant was located in the yards 1,687 feet due south of the Headhouse on the center line of the trainshed. Atop the power house and occupying its north front facing the Station track system was the Interlocking or Signal Tower, whose operations controlled the movement of all trains into and out of the shed. Later, when a major rearrangement of the track system into the shed was made, eliminating the original "single-throat" track approach in favor of a "double-throat" system, the power plant was relocated along the Eighteenth Street side of the approach yard. The Interlocking Tower was then rebuilt near its original location and two more tracks were added under the trainshed.

Also during the 1890s, four express company buildings occupied an area south of the trainshed and between the shed tracks and Eighteenth Street. These too, were removed at the time of the trackage rearrangement.

The western side of the trainshed also presented a different appearance when the Station was new. Here was a two-story building, 30 feet wide and 300 feet long, called the Baggage Room building. Most of its lower floor was used for baggage transfer purposes, while its upper floor contained offices, storage rooms, and accommodations for railroad conductors. It was located under the shed along Twentieth Street, just south of the Midway. Further south and also under the western edge of the shed was another two-story structure occupied by the United States Post Office mail facility. These two buildings were designed to integrate the baggage and mail operations more closely to the trains than had been possible previously.

After Union Station had been in operation for several years, it became obvious that operational adjustments were needed, especially in view of potential traffic demands that would be generated by the impending St. Louis World's Fair in 1904. A two-year program of improvement was begun in 1902. This included the new "double-throat" track approach, removal of the express buildings to a new location along Twentieth Street, and extension of the trainshed by 180 feet. A new signal control tower was added, but unfortunately it burned during the World's Fair year. (It was rebuilt, but the new tower was also destroyed by fire on July 22, 1940. The newest control tower was placed in operation on October 8, 1940.) As expected, the World's Fair was a substantial but successful test of Union Station's efficiency. A spe-

The switch tower or signal tower (c. 1895) was the nerve center of the station. Train engineers were obliged to seek clearance from the controllers here before proceeding into the trainshed.

In the 1890s thousands of valises, grips, trunks, and carpetbags were rounded up and sorted at the western end of the trainshed.

St. Louis Globe-Democrat / St. Louis Public Library

**Mr. ZIP, circa 1945: tunnels between Union Station and the Post Office allowed the mail to bypass the throngs above. Here, a postal worker has the road to himself.**

cial shuttle service was inaugurated to take visitors directly from the Station to the Fair. It ran on Terminal and Wabash tracks to a special Wabash station at the Fair's main entrance.

While the use of Union Station was still on the upswing, a new extension to the west of the main trainshed added a two-story baggage building of stone at Market and relocated Twentieth Street in 1929. This annex added 10 more tracks to the Station, bringing its total to 42. New umbrella-type platform shelters were used in place of an overhead shed. This addition reinforced Union Station's claim of having the greatest number of tracks on one level of any railroad station in the world.

Also in 1929, heating of the Midway was begun, much to the delight of travelers who considered its 720-foot expanse the coldest place in town. Other Midway changes included the removal of a stairway to the Grand Hall in 1937, and the construction of a tunnel to a parking lot across Twentieth Street. In the yards beyond the trainshed, a new mail-handling shed was located, out where mail and express cars were loaded and unloaded. This was connected to the Post Office and Railway Express building across Eighteenth Street by long tunnels under the trainshed. These were reached from the platform level by elevators from the mail facility.

In more recent years, the greatest pressure upon the facilities of Union Station occurred during World War II. Most of the movement of troops, recruits, and other service men and women was done by rail, and the central location of St. Louis attracted a formidable number of trains for military use, besides an increased volume of civilian rail traffic. In the mid-war year of 1943, 1,347,998 tickets were sold at the modern Union Station ticket offices. During that year, the Fred Harvey restaurants served meals to 2,714,570 hungry travelers. Fred Harvey also operated a cafeteria in the Station and the upstairs Dining Hall, for the exclusive use of military men and women traveling on government order.

On the second or main floor, to the west of the richly frescoed Grand Hall, was the popular and comfortable U.S.O. Lounge, used intensively by service men and women during and after World War II. Ample facilities for reading, writing, relaxing, and sampling refreshments were available.

Across the Grand Hall, on its eastern side, was a large Ladies' Lounge, a pleasant place in which to relax between trains. Especially appreciated by wives and children of service men was a Nursery equipped with everything needed for the care of children. It was operated by the American Women's Voluntary Services under the supervi-

St. Louis Post-Dispatch

**In the 1940s, servicemen making cross-country connections beseiged the Union Station Information Desk.**

St. Louis Globe-Democrat

**Eventually, special desks were set up to handle military reservations.**

St. Louis Post-Dispatch

# THE WAR YEARS
# 1941-1945

**A young mother threads her way through wartime crowds on the Midway.**

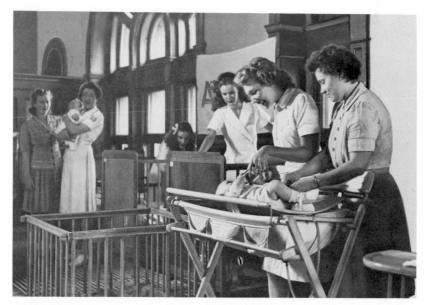

**Mullanphy's Travelers Aid volunteers, in cooperation with the U.S.O., staff a nursery during the war years to give beleaguered parents a break from tending their little ones.**

sion of Mullanphy Travelers Aid. That organization was founded before the Civil War, from a bequest of Bryan Mullanphy, a St. Louis philanthropist. It was intended to aid travelers going westward to the frontier, and has continued since to help stranded or bewildered strangers suffering from the adversities of travel. It maintained a bureau in Union Station for many years.

During the war years, 300 persons were required to handle the volume of baggage and mail at the Union Station, which reached its wartime peak in 1943, when 72,621 trains, 660,000 cars, and 22 million passengers were cleared through the terminal. Wartime reservations and telephone queries were handled by a newly built Central Reservation Bureau located above the Eighteenth Street entrance to the Station.

There is a natural parallel between the demise of Union Station and the dramatic decline of railroad passenger traffic. During the late 1950s, when railroads were dropping passenger trains on a nationwide scale, critics charged them with not properly merchandising passenger travel and with intentionally using obsolete equipment. The railroads claimed that passenger rail traffic did not pull its weight financially, that it was subsidized by freight operations. However, another factor in the passenger train situation over which the railroads had no control was increasing competition from other modes of transportation. The automobile was the number one villain in the piece, and the airplane was number two. A historical comparison reveals the extent of their inroads.

In 1900, railroads carried 84 percent of all intercity passengers; most of the remainder went by boat. But when the auto came into its own in the 1920s the picture began to change. By 1954 the travel volume had reached the opposite pole, with 88 percent of all travelers going by private automobile. After that, the coup de grace was delivered by the inauguration of the Interstate Highway System in 1956, with its spreading network of limited-access intercity superhighways. It became possible to drive hundreds of miles without being impeded by traffic lights, and to bypass slowdowns in cities and towns. With this freedom of movement, the efficient automobile and its spinoff, the bus, took an increasing bite out of railroad passenger volume, which had fallen to five percent of the national travel total. At that time airlines accounted for most of the remaining portion. From the 1950s on, most travelers on long trips or those needing a fast and reliable way to go preferred the airlines.

One of the valid complaints by the railroads was that their highway and air competition had the benefit of federal subsidies for the construction of roads and airports, while the railroads had to maintain

Union Pacific System

In the days before the amplification device shown here, a train caller was hired for the power of his lungs.

Wayne Leeman

In 1957 four men were needed to operate the intricate switching console. The overhead panel shows all tracks leading to the Station.

With expert choreography, switchmen guided hundreds of trains in and out of
Union Station on a huge web of tracks.

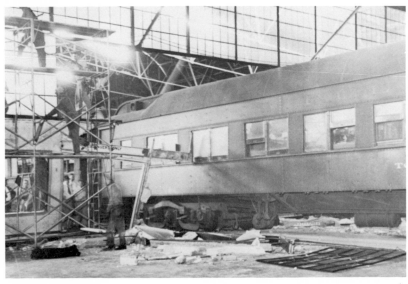

It finally happened! On September 7, 1943, a Wabash Railroad train with a
Pullman tourist sleeper backed into the Midway.

their own yards, rights-of-way, and tracks.

In St. Louis, Union Station's greatest peacetime year was 1920, when more than 93,000 trains moved in and out of its trainshed, an average of about 269 daily. After a brief surge during World War II, the number of trains handled here annually dropped to 53,672, or about 147 per day, in 1950. Seven years later these figures dropped further, this time to about 42,000 a year (115 per day). This decline continued into the 1970s, when railroad use of Union Station was virtually abandoned.

A contributing factor to the heavy traffic in the Station during the 1920s was the 35 commuter or "accommodation" trains operated on the Frisco, Missouri Pacific, and Wabash railroads. They carried about half a million passengers annually between Union Station and various suburban depots. The last commuter train run was made by the Mo Pac's *Pacific Eagle* on December 15, 1961.

When train travel was in its heyday, the Pullman Company operated 120 cars daily through Union Station. But by November 1967, that total had fallen to 12. In that year, Missouri Pacific dropped its passenger trains between St. Louis and Kansas City, and only 14 trains left the Station daily. This spectacular decline in the railroad use of Union Station left most of its tracks vacant and unused. Consequently, many of them were removed during the 1970s.

Union Station's last railroad tenant was the National Railroad Passenger Corporation, a federal government agency organized to administer the passenger system. Its rail network, originally called Railpax when it was established on January 1, 1970, was later renamed Amtrak.

When it assumed operation of the nation's passenger railroad traffic on May 1, 1971, it had three trains daily running through St. Louis. Two of them ran to Chicago and Milwaukee, while the third operated between New York and Kansas City. The latter train, called the *National Limited*, was discontinued on July 1, 1973. Meanwhile, Amtrak announced its desire to vacate Union Station and build a new station elsewhere. In June 1975, plans for a new Amtrak station at Scott and Ewing avenues were publicized. Construction of the $1.7 million project was to have begun early in 1976.

Despite the T.R.R.A.'s sale of Union Station, Amtrak still had Interstate Commerce Commission permission to use the Station. Later, Amtrak abandoned the Scott-Ewing site as too remote and began considering a proposal by Wallace A. Wright, Jr., the new developer for Union Center Venture, to house Amtrak in the old Railway Express Agency building at Eighteenth Street and Clark Avenue. Finally in 1978,

Amtrak decided to leave Union Station and to build a "temporary" station at 550 South Sixteenth Street. Accordingly, the last train out of Union Station, an Amtrak train to Chicago, left the historic edifice on October 31, 1978.

Since then, Amtrak has been urged by several potential developers of Union Station to return its operations there. Amtrak also had plans to replace its "trailer" depot, but could not erect a permanent station because of a lack of funds. Amtrak's uncertainty caused delays in the progressive planning for the new Union Station project. However, in 1983 Amtrak proposed building a new station across Twentieth Street, west of Union Station and separate from it.

Ridership on Amtrak's two trains between St. Louis and Kansas City—the *Ann Rutledge*, which runs through St. Louis on its way from Chicago to Kansas City, and the *Missouri Mule*, from St. Louis to Kansas City—reached a record in September 1983. This figure of 6,860 passengers represented a 17 percent increase over the previous year and was the best September since the inception of Amtrak in 1971. The fiscal year ending September 30, 1983, showed a 12 percent gain over the previous year. During the 1982-83 fiscal year the state of Missouri paid Amtrak $1.7 million to operate the trains, which represented 65 percent of its operational costs. The St. Louis–Kansas City route that year was one of the most traveled in the Amtrak System, which had registered no net increase nationally. On the basis of the Missouri trains' performance, Amtrak recently approved an extension route from St. Louis to Centralia, Illinois, to connect with trains from Chicago to New Orleans.

As early as 1945, alternative future uses for Union Station were being discussed. At that time, a St. Louis alderman proposed converting it into a transportation center for trains and buses, with adjacent landing strips for aircraft. In those days it was thought that the reversible-pitch propeller would make airline traffic into downtown areas practical. In 1958, Mayor Raymond R. Tucker appointed a commission to study the redevelopment of Union Station as a transport center with shuttle helicopter service to Lambert–St. Louis Municipal Airport. But the plan failed when Greyhound Bus Lines showed no interest in locating its station there.

A variety of alternative uses were proposed in 1965 following a meeting of the League of Women Voters at the Station. Such diverse ideas as a branch art museum, a concert hall, a natural history museum, and a shopping center were suggested. During the late 1960s a serious effort was made to house the National Museum of Transport under the Station's cavernous trainshed.

Railroad hobbyists and fans heed the final "all aboard." Union Station's last train pulled out on October 31, 1978.

St. Louis Globe-Democrat

Jazz musicians play a funeral dirge.

St. Louis Globe-Democrat

Lucille Linebach

**The redcap class of 1916 saw plenty of action. Ray O'Neill (center) eventually became Stationmaster and retired after more than 50 years of service.**

In 1968, McDonnell-Douglas Corporation suggested that a short takeoff and landing (STOL) airport might be built just south of Union Station, and it conducted simulated landings there. However, this idea came to naught because Mayor Alfonso J. Cervantes was committed to a plan for a convention center, amusement park, hotel and shop complex for Union Station. This idea was abandoned when Six Flags, Inc., decided to build their new amusement park in St. Louis County. So upon its seventy-fifth anniversary in 1969, Union Station was in a quandary.

Confirmation of Union Station's architectural importance came when it was declared to be a St. Louis Landmark in 1966 and was placed upon the National Register of Historic Places in 1970. During the summer of 1973, St. Louis was rife with reports that the Terminal Railroad Association was considering the sale of Union Station to a Miami developer. This speculation was confirmed in October 1973, when Harry Gurwitch, president of a Miami investment firm, announced ambitious plans for the rehabilitation of Union Station and its vicinity.

On July 16, 1974, it was announced that the T.R.R.A. had sold Union Station for $2.5 million to the Union Center Venture, which consisted of three partners. These were Gurwitch; Bruce Paul, a Denver lawyer; and James O. Holton, a St. Louis bank president. Along with the sale announcement, Gurwitch stated that his original plans were "too specific" and would be modified. It was also said that they were looking for a nationally known developer for the project. Delays in the project's progress were later blamed on the tight money market.

In late 1974, Theatre Project Company began to present its plays in Union Station's remodeled ladies' waiting room. After a long period of inactivity, Union Center Venture announced on December 28, 1975, that Wallace A. Wright, Jr., developer of Salt Lake City's famed Trolley Square, had become a partner in the venture. By April 1977, Wright had devised a $51 million plan for Union Center Venture and had obtained approval by the city of St. Louis for its important 25-year tax-abatement feature. But Wright was still negotiating with Amtrak as to whether it would develop a station in the old Railway Express Agency building. Wright's controversy with Amtrak caused litigation and prevented him from obtaining major tenant commitments for the project. In 1978, Wright was also seeking new equity partners because the original three investors had withdrawn. Convincing financial institutions that the renovation project was feasible was also a problem.

In October 1978, the shaky financial status of the Union Center Venture brought a threat from the Colorado Federal Savings and Loan Association of Denver to raze Union Station as a last resort to recover the money loaned for the project. It had also begun foreclosure proceedings against Union Center Venture, which had fallen behind in mortgage payments on the $4 million loan. The loan firm indicated that it would put the Station property up for sale during the next month. (The Amtrak problem was solved in November 1978, when it finally vacated the Station.)

On March 1, 1979, Oppenheimer Properties, Inc., of New York announced plans to purchase the Station property from Union Center Venture, which then consisted of Wright and some other partners. It took more than a year to close the deal. St. Louis Station Associates became the local representatives of Oppenheimer on the project.

In September 1980, Oppenheimer announced that it had hired the Rouse Company of Columbia, Maryland, to develop the project. Rouse, one of the nation's leading real estate developers, operates 59 retail projects in the United States and Canada. Among these are Fanueil Hall Marketplace in Boston, Harborplace in Baltimore, and South Street Seaport in New York City.

A major financial hurdle for the St. Louis Union Station project was cleared in September 1982, when the federal Department of Housing and Urban Development announced approval of a $10 million grant to the city of St. Louis, which in turn loaned it to the St. Louis Station Associates for a start on construction in 1983. This grant helped toward the $135 million needed to finance the St. Louis Union Station project. It reportedly included multimillion dollar investments by the developers, banks, and private sources. Aiding in the financing were investment tax credits allowed under the federal Economic Recovery Act, because St. Louis Union Station was on the National Register of Historic Places and the project represented a substantial certified rehabilitation. A "commencement" ceremony for the St. Louis Union Station redevelopment occurred in the Station's Grand Hall on July 21, 1983. Opening ceremonies for the Station project were held on August 29, 1985, when the former railroad station was reopened as a specialty retail/luxury hotel/entertainment complex. The Station's Grand Hall was restored to its earlier grandeur to serve as the lobby for a 550-room luxury hotel, which includes the area formerly occupied by the old Terminal Hotel and a portion of the trainshed area to the south. The hotel is operated by Omni International, which runs luxury hotels in Atlanta, Miami, Boston, and several other cities.

The busy Midway has been converted into a climate-controlled area with boutiques, retail kiosks, and eateries. The adjoining former trainshed area has been partially reroofed to house restaurants, specialty retail shops, a fountain, and part of the hotel. Adjoining the hotel in this

After seven years of silence, Union Station burst into life again on Aug. 30, 1985.

Rouse Company of St. Louis

area is a one-acre lake, which brings St. Louis Union Station full-circle from the time 150 years ago when its site was an arm of Chouteau's Pond. Architecturally, no changes have been made to the Station's historic Romanesque facade or clock tower. Inside, major portions of the Headhouse now appear as they did when it was new. The Station's interior had been redecorated over the years and had lost much of its original luster.

Meticulous research and skilled craftsmanship were used to restore the original concept. Paint was stripped down to the first coat, stencils were uncovered and restored, new gold-leaf was applied, and scagliola—plaster designed to resemble marble—was recreated. The allegorical stained-glass window over the Grand Hall staircase entrance, which had suffered from buckling and breakage, was removed, releaded, and reglazed where necessary with matching colored antique glass. All other stained-glass windows have also been restored.

In the American Rotisserie, Omni International Hotel's signature restaurant, much of the woodwork had been covered with a dark varnish, and during the 1940s the wood in the Grand Hall had been refinished in a bright yellow. This has been stripped and refinished in its original honey-colored oak. The zigzag borders of the mosaic-looking encaustic tiles have been repaired to match their English originals. Opalescent swirled-glass light fixtures in the Gothic Corridor, which had disappeared, were replaced with new ones shipped from Europe. Sculpture, decorative plaster, and bas-relief restorations have been completed. The magnificent St. Louis Union Station Headhouse once again reflects its remarkable Romanesque style, just as designer Louis Millet created it in 1894.

The spirit of a city within a city, for which St. Louis Union Station was well known, has been recaptured in its renaissance. More than 160,000 square feet of retail space, plus kiosks and pushcarts, offers a wide variety from fine apparel to the unique and unusual. The Pullman Market features fresh flowers and produce as well as specialty foods. Strolling performers, museum exhibits, crafts demonstrations, and other attractions provide constant entertainment. And the Station's landscaped park with its lake, sparkling fountains, walkways, and glass elevators offers strolling and people-watching opportunities, too. The Omni International Hotel, providing 550 world-class luxury rooms, in addition to a variety of dining experiences, furnishes both guests and shoppers with numerous unique and elegant occasions. Convenient parking space is provided for 2,000 cars. This $135 million redevelopment has been called the largest "adaptive reuse" project in the United States.

As a spinoff from the St. Louis Union Station improvements, local planners foresee a demand for office and commerical space in new or existing structures in the surrounding neighborhood. Civic projects have had a major influence in creating an attractive environment around Union Station.

Across Market Street opposite the Station is Aloe Plaza, opened in 1931 and named for a former president of the Board of Aldermen. In 1940, the fountain and statuary called "The Meeting of the Waters," by Swedish sculptor Carl Milles, were added to Aloe Plaza. The fountain group of 14 bronze figures represents the union of the Mississippi and Missouri rivers just north of St. Louis.

Such environmental assets and the great work in St. Louis Union Station should prove to be mutually beneficial to its owners and to the city of St. Louis.

St. Louis Post-Dispatch

**Mrs. Louis P. Aloe confers with sculptor Carl Milles as two neighborhood children admire their work. Mrs. Aloe donated the fountain in memory of her late husband.**

# PART II

*The Railroads
Serving St. Louis
and their
Development*

**Terminal Railroad Association
switch crews pose at the neck
of the "Y" in 1895.**

Railroad developments in the United States began in the first states along the Atlantic seaboard, principally in New England and southward to Maryland, Virginia, and the Carolinas. The idea of hauling goods on rails originated in England and had spread to this country by the second decade of the nineteenth century. Major cities on the Atlantic coast became centers for many short-line railroads that were later linked up into more extensive systems. They soon undermined the commercial value of turnpikes and canals.

Westward access toward the Mississippi River and the Great Lakes was pushed along three major rail routes; the New York Central through the Mohawk Valley, the Pennsylvania across the mountains toward Pittsburgh, and the Baltimore & Ohio along the Potomac and the Ohio River Valley. The latter two railroads eventually reached the Mississippi opposite St. Louis as, respectively, the Vandalia line in 1870 and the Ohio & Mississippi Railroad in 1857.

St. Louis became acquainted with railroad operation through the demonstration of a miniature railway in August 1830 at the old Baptist church at Third and Market streets. A steam locomotive pulled a car, seating one person, around a 100-foot circular track at a speed of seven miles per hour.

Enthusiasm for railroads increased here during the early 1830s, following favorable reports of new railroad lines in the Eastern states. This culminated in a convention at the Courthouse on April 26, 1836, where plans were proposed for two railroads from St. Louis—one to Fayette, Missouri, and the other to the mineral-rich southeastern section of the state. Federal and state aid was sought for construction and political support was obtained. The State Assembly chartered 18 railroad companies, but failed to appropriate any funds because of a lack of revenue. Subsequently, the Panic of 1837 put any grandiose railroad schemes to rest for some years.

The decade of the 1840s was marked by continued press agitation for railroads. However, the movement was stifled by political differences. Some favored federal aid and state subsidies, but conservatives opposed the state's going into debt, even for such progressive purposes as railroad construction.

The earliest of all railroads in the St. Louis area was built by a predecessor of the Illinois and St. Louis Coal Company to mines on the Illinois bluffs in 1836. This short line was also the first railroad to be built in Illinois; it used horses for its means of locomotion. Further railroad construction in the low-lying bottomland on the east side of the Mississippi was delayed by serious floods in 1844 and 1853. The only means of access to St. Louis from the east side was by ferry boats, principally by the Wiggins Ferry Company, which was established in 1818 and began using steam power in 1828.

Among the railroad charters granted in Missouri in January 1837 were ones for the St. Louis and Bellevue Mineral Railroad Company and the Louisiana and Columbia Railroad Company. Because of a lack of financing, neither of these was built then, but they were constructed during the 1850s as parts of other lines. The former was included in the St. Louis & Iron Mountain Railroad charter in 1851, while the latter was incorporated into the Hannibal & St. Joseph Railroad. A Missouri state board of improvements, created in 1840, made a survey for a railroad route from St. Louis to the Iron Mountain by way of the Big River.

Interest of St. Louisans in connecting the city with Boston by rail led to a town meeting in June 1839, but the project failed to materialize. In the next year a railroad convention was held in St. Louis at the National Hotel, with similar results. By the late 1840s, when Missouri had become more prosperous and populous, interest in railroads was revived on a broader basis. Federal aid for railroads was requested in a "memorial to Congress" in 1847. The awareness of Missourians of the necessity for a system of public works to take advantage of the natural resources in the state was emphasized. Two objectives were stressed. One concerned the chartering of a railroad to connect the Mississippi and Missouri rivers between Hannibal and St. Joseph. (For financial support the legislature suggested that the federal government could contribute alternate sections of public land along the route.) Secondly, the memorial proposed surveying and developing railroads to utilize the rich mineral resources in southeastern Missouri.

While the document accentuated the developmental needs of Missouri, the principal beneficiary of such a program would have been the city of St. Louis. Civic leaders in St. Louis were envious of accomplishments in Illinois, where the Illinois and Michigan Canal was opened and railroads were built into Chicago from the east and west. Pressure was exerted on Missouri state legislators for railroad bills when it was realized that St. Louis could not rely upon river traffic indefinitely. However, the legislature refused to nullify a law that distributed Missouri's improvement funds to every county in the state, to the disadvantage of St. Louis.

The good life on the Missouri Pacific Railroad in the 1880s featured berths, parlor cars, and musicales.

# THE PACIFIC RAILROAD AND THE MISSOURI PACIFIC

During the 1840s, various suggestions were made for the construction of a railroad to link St. Louis with the Pacific Coast. Articles on that subject appeared in the *Western Journal* in December 1848. The idea received impetus on February 7, 1849, when Senator Thomas Hart Benton presented his plan for a Pacific railroad to the United States Senate. Soon thereafter, prominent St. Louisans held a meeting to further the project. It culminated in the grant of a charter by the Missouri legislature for the Pacific Railroad on March 12, 1849. Chartered as the Pacific Railroad of Missouri, this corporation was given the right to construct a railroad from St. Louis to the western boundary of Missouri, to join there with any railroad which should be built eastward from the Pacific Coast.

Railroad enthusiasm in St. Louis was kindled by a series of meetings during the spring and summer of 1849 to elect delegates to a railroad convention that was to be held at the St. Louis Courthouse on October 15, 1849. This convention crystalized public sentiment in favor of railroad construction generally and for a railway from the Mississippi River to the Pacific Ocean specifically. The latter support was achieved through the ardent oratory of Senator Benton. At a later meeting, called by civic leader Thomas Allen, 11 prominent St. Louisans pledged to buy 1,540 shares of stock in the Pacific Railroad at $100 per share. By four months after the convention, $319,000 had been raised locally to underwrite the project.

In January 1850, the railroad's incorporators met in St. Louis to complete its organization. They were prominent public-spirited citizens under the leadership of Allen and Colonel John O'Fallon, who was chosen as the company's first president. Soon thereafter, O'Fallon was replaced by Allen, who served his first year without pay.

Although spurred by concern over the increasing competition from Chicago, the railroad company encountered difficulty in financing its objective. Aid was sought from the federal and state governments, and pledges were made by cities and towns along the line's proposed route. These were opened by a $500,000 bond purchase by St. Louis County in 1850 that was approved in an election by a ten-to-one vote. Within a short time practically every county along the route had approved some form of assistance for the railroad. However, many of these pledges later proved difficult to collect. Some required prolonged litigation, and amounts due on the bonds were frequently compromised in order to secure payments.

While financial support was being sought, actual work on the railroad was started. Surveys began in May 1850 under the direction of James P. Kirkwood, formerly of the New York & Erie Railroad, who had been hired as general manager of the Pacific. The route finally adopted followed the Missouri River closely as far as Jefferson City, and then struck out straight across the state toward Kansas City. With this physical progress under way, enthusiasm was generated, leading to more support for the project. While various surveys were still being considered, there was increased interest competitively among towns along the proposed routes. Surveying had progressed sufficiently by the summer of 1851 to allow construction to begin.

Ground was broken at St. Louis by Mayor Luther M. Kennett on July 4, 1851, for the start of the first railroad west of the Mississippi. The ceremonies were held on the south shore of Chouteau's Pond near the present intersection of Sixteenth Street and Chouteau Avenue. It was a festive and momentous occasion for St. Louisans, preceded by a parade and followed by oratory and refreshments—punch served from a farmer's well.

Ironically, the railroad's first locomotive arrived at St. Louis aboard a steamboat from New Orleans, after it had made a trip by sea from the factory in Massachusetts. After its arrival on August 20, 1852, the iron horse was put into service for the first time in December 1852 on a trip to the end of the line. This was the first train to be operated from St. Louis, and due to the slowness of construction work the track ended only five miles out at Cheltenham, now Sulphur Avenue. It was not until 1855 that the main line reached Jefferson City. Due to interruptions by the Civil War the track to Kansas City was not finally completed until 1865. A southwestern branch line to Rolla was completed in 1861.

Completion of the railroad to the state capital was an occasion for special celebration, which unfortunately ended in abject tragedy. A long train of 14 cars, loaded with civic and railroad dignitaries, caused the disastrous collapse of a bridge over the Gasconade River on November 1, 1885. When the train reached the first pier, the bridge collapsed, sending the locomotive and ten cars down a 30-foot embankment. Twenty-five persons were killed or mortally injured.

Despite such setbacks, railroad enthusiasm during the 1850s rode a tide of favorable sentiment in Congress. After a major grant to the Illinois Central Railroad in 1850, a consistent Congressional policy of aid by grants of land to the western states was followed. Missouri was given a land grant on June 10, 1852, which embraced all even-numbered sections within six miles of the proposed railroad from St. Louis to the state's western boundary and from Hannibal to St. Joseph. The drawback was that the land depended upon completion of the line for its value and was therefore of little financial assistance during the construction period. In December 1852, the Missouri Legislature voted another million dollars in state aid for the Pacific Railroad. Even so, the final cost greatly exceeded the original estimates and the project was in constant financial difficulty. Completed by July 19, 1853, the first division, a distance of 37 miles to the town of Pacific, cost $1,769,874, or about $47,000 per mile. By late 1864 interest in the Pacific Railroad was revived sufficiently to enable its completion to Kansas City by the end of 1865. After going into receivership in 1876, the Pacific Railroad was reorganized as the Missouri Pacific Railroad Company.

Increasing competition among midwestern railroads indicated a need for some form of cooperation at this time. One example was unified action to solve the problem of poor rail connections caused by a lack of time standards. This cooperation led to the adoption of standard time nationally in the early 1880s. A new standard of elegance was achieved by the Missouri Pacific in the early 1880s, when it announced new "palace chair cars" on its express trains. No extra charge was made for seats in these cars. The company advertised that "no other line runs these cars between St. Louis and Kansas City."

Meanwhile on the St. Louis scene, local "accommodation trains" began operating on the Pacific Railroad during the early 1870s. They ran to suburban stations such as Kirkwood and were predecessors of the later commuter trains. In 1887, the St. Louis, Oak Hill, and Carondelet branch line was opened between the Missouri Pacific lines at Tower Grove and the Iron Mountain tracks in Carondelet. Popularly called the Oak Hill branch, this line had a considerable impact on the growth of southwest St. Louis. At Lake Junction, east of Webster Groves, a branch line to Creve Coeur Lake joins the main line of the Missouri Pacific. This branch, completed in 1891, allowed ice cut at the lake to be shipped to St. Louis. Passenger service on this ten-mile branch was ended in 1929.

The Missouri Pacific and Iron Mountain railroads were declared bankrupt after a default in August 1915, and were placed in receivership by the federal court. They were reorganized on March 5, 1917, and merged into the Missouri Pacific Railroad Company, ending the corporate structure of the St. Louis, Iron Mountain & Southern.

In an expansion of its commuter service, the Missouri Pacific put six new suburban trains into operation between St. Louis and Kirkwood in 1923. One was a *Shopper's Special*, added at the request of residents of Webster Groves and Kirkwood.

Lewis W. Baldwin became president of the Missouri Pacific in 1923. One of his projects, the acquisition of the Gulf Coast Lines and the International & Great Northern, was accomplished on January 1, 1925.

In May 1928, Missouri Pacific moved to its new 22-story general office building at Thirteenth and Olive streets in downtown St. Louis, after vacating several floors in the Railway Exchange Building. The new building became a progressive symbol and an important factor in the railroad's public image.

Diesel passenger locomotives powered Mo Pac's first lightweight streamlined train, the *Missouri River Eagle,* in 1940. About the same time, air-conditioning was added on the *Sunshine Special*, Missouri Pacific's crack passenger train to the Southwest. Wartime restrictions caused the replacement of the *Scenic Limited* by the diesel-powered *Colorado Eagles* in the St. Louis–to–Denver service in June 1942. Within four years the *Eagles* ran 2,616,904 miles and had carried more than two million passengers. A casualty of the war period was the dropping of all but one of the St. Louis suburban commuter trains in late 1940.

Extensive grade and line revisions were made on the Missouri Division south of St. Louis after 1946. This was part of a long-range program to improve the main line for the introduction of the high-speed *Texas Eagles*. They replaced the famous *Sunshine Special* in August 1948.

A major milestone in the history of the Missouri Pacific was the centennial of the founding of its predecessor, the Pacific Railroad, which was the first railroad west of the Mississippi. The centennial, on July 4, 1951, was celebrated with a dinner under the auspices of the

Missouri Historical Society at the Hotel Chase, and the introduction of new dining car chinaware bearing historical scenes.

With a bow to progress in April 1955, the steam era ended on the Missouri Pacific. At that time, the last of its steam locomotives was moved to Dupo, Illinois, for disposal as scrap.

Passenger service on the Mo Pac gradually declined. In 1971, when Amtrak began, some of its trains ran on Mo Pac tracks. On April 18, 1980, stockholders of the Missouri Pacific and the Union Pacific Corporations approved a merger by which Mo Pac became part of the Union Pacific System. The two railroads were to be affiliated companies. The merger, which also included the Western Pacific Railroad Company in a 22,800-mile system serving 21 states, was finalized with approval of the Interstate Commerce Commission late in 1982. As a result of this merger, the original Pacific Railroad concept was achieved by a direct connection on proprietary tracks to the Pacific Coast.

A *Sunshine Special* ad suggests that truly fashionable people wouldn't travel any other way.

# THE ST. LOUIS, IRON MOUNTAIN & SOUTHERN RAILWAY

From the earliest days of railroad enthusiasm in Missouri, the need for a rail connection southward from St. Louis to the rich iron and lead deposits in the southeastern part of the state was well recognized. One of the first railroad charters granted in Missouri was for the St. Louis and Bellevue Mineral Railroad on January 25, 1837.

A survey for its route made by W. H. Morrell in 1839 was the first west of the Mississippi. Later surveys were made in 1849 and 1852 for the St. Louis & Iron Mountain Railroad, which included the Bellevue line in its charter of March 3, 1851. This charter provided for capital stock of $6 million and gave the St. Louis & Iron Mountain Railroad Company authority to build a line from St. Louis to the Iron Mountain region. It also gave the company the right to extend its tracks to Cape Girardeau and to the southwestern part of Missouri within ten years. Its St. Louis depot was at Fourth and Plum streets after 1857.

On December 25, 1852, the state granted the Pacific Railroad Company authority to build the Iron Mountain branch and its extensions, and it created a state credit of $750,000 for that purpose. The Iron Mountain Company was organized on November 4, 1852, and construction began in the fall of 1853.

The first locomotive was operated in 1856, but the railroad did not open the full line for business to Pilot Knob until May 11, 1858. This long delay was due to difficulties encountered during various stages of the line's construction. Soon after the first rail was laid, it became apparent that the work had been awarded to unscrupulous contractors, so the company had to cancel the contracts and complete the work itself. Although the railroad followed a U.S. government survey route along the Mississippi southward from St. Louis, the War Department imposed restrictions on trains operating through the St. Louis Arsenal grounds, the grounds of the U.S. Marine Hospital, and Jefferson Barracks. They contended that the trains operating through the properties should be pulled by mules to avoid the fire hazards created by sparks from the wood-burning locomotives. Congressional action was required to overcome this objection.

By 1855, track was completed between the Arsenal and Carondelet. A year later a detached service was begun with an "omnibus train," so-called because passengers from St. Louis had to take a horse-drawn omnibus to reach a temporary railroad station at Lami Street before proceeding to Carondelet by train. Full service was initiated in 1858.

Extensive railroad machine shops were built at Carondelet in 1859, and the new railroad soon became heavily used for commuter traffic and for freight hauling, especially transporting iron ore to smelters in Carondelet. On the St. Louis scene, a unique "cliffhanger" railroad station was built by the Iron Mountain line at Itaska Street. It perched on the side of the river bluff and was reached from trackside by a steep flight of steps. Other local stations were at Davis, Robert, Krauss, and Elwood streets. Trip time from Elwood to the Union Depot was 40 minutes in 1890.

An employees' hospital, opened by the Iron Mountain Railroad in 1880 in the former Blow mansion at Virginia and Loughborough avenues in Carondelet, was the forerunner of the Missouri Pacific Hospital, located at 1600 California Avenue from 1884 to 1922. Mo Pac eventually severed its relations with the hospital, which moved to a new building at 1755 South Grand Boulevard in 1923. It was later known as the Compton Hill Medical Center.

After the opening of the Oak Hill branch in 1889, which gave Iron Mountain trains eventual access to Union Station, passenger stations were built along the branch in Carondelet Park and at other locations to serve commuters. A particularly busy station was the one at South Broadway and Tesson Street, which opened in 1902. A timetable of 1907 shows that 15 trains stopped there daily. By 1964, it was abandoned, as were many others, including the Mo Pac station at Tower Grove Avenue. Competition from local transit caused a cessation of commuter services on the Oak Hill branch and along the river route to downtown.

On January 16, 1906, a successful semiweekly passenger train through service was inaugurated on the Iron Mountain during the winter season between St. Louis and Mexico City.

In an expansion action in September 1909, the Iron Mountain purchased 13 subsidiary railroad companies with a trackage totaling 759 miles. But on August 19, 1915, the Iron Mountain and the Missouri Pacific went into default and were declared bankrupt and under a receivership by the federal court.

The Iron Mountain Railroad merged with the Missouri Pacific on March 5, 1917, and was reorganized into a new company, the Missouri Pacific Railroad Company, after which the corporate structure of the Iron Mountain Railroad ceased to exist.

Engine Number 144 was built in 1881 by Grant Locomotive Works. The Iron Mountain eventually merged its gleaming rolling stock and trackage with that of the Missouri Pacific Railroad Company.

# Mississippi River & Bonne Terre Railway

One short-line Missouri railroad that ran passenger trains into St. Louis Union Station was the Mississippi River & Bonne Terre Railway. It was built in 1890 from Doe Run, Missouri, to a junction with the Iron Mountain Railroad at Riverside, one mile south of Herculaneum. It was primarily a freight line for the St. Joseph Lead Company, which had its headquarters in Bonne Terre, and for a subsidiary, the Doe Run Lead Company. The railway had a length of 46.4 miles from Doe Run through Bonne Terre to Riverside, and had a total of 64 miles of track in 1925.

During December 1920, the MR&BT operated four passenger trains daily at St. Louis Union Station. It was later absorbed by the Missouri-Illinois Railroad, a subsidiary of the Missouri Pacific.

# St. Louis & San Franciso Railway— Frisco Lines

Among the routes proposed to connect St. Louis with the Pacific Coast by rail was one that would run along the Thirty-fifth Parallel. It was believed that trains could travel relatively snow-free to Southern California, and then strike northward to San Francisco. The first attempt was the provision for a southwest branch of the Pacific Railroad.

This Southwest Branch was endowed by the state of Missouri with 1,200,000 acres of land and a million dollars in state bonds in December 1852. Although a contract for construction was signed in 1853, actual work did not begin until June 1855. Delay was caused by the same financial troubles which plagued the Pacific Railroad during this period. By the onset of the Civil War, the Branch was completed to Rolla, 75 miles southwest of Franklin. There it remained during the war, while efforts were made to counteract the damage sustained from marauding bands of outlaws who terrorized the state at that time. Their depredations were so serious that both the Branch and the main line Pacific Railroad were bankrupt by the end of the war.

In 1866 the Branch was purchased by General John C. Fremont and associates; however, the line reached only to the Gasconade River during Fremont's regime. A new company was formed in 1868, subject to completion to the western boundary of Missouri in 1872. This was accomplished about a year earlier. In 1876, the line was reorganized as the St. Louis & San Francisco Railway Company, including acquisition of the Pacific Railroad's Southwest Branch. At that time the railroad acquired its "Frisco" nickname because extension to the Golden Gate seemed a possibility. However, the Indians continued to block work on the line through the Indian Territory, and in 1879 control of the Frisco was acquired by the Santa Fe Railway, which used the A&P franchise to build its own line from Albuquerque, New Mexico, to California.

After its separation from the Missouri Pacific, the Frisco was forced to pay for the privilege of running its trains from Pacific into St. Louis on Mo Pac tracks. This compelled the Frisco to build its own line into St. Louis in 1883 along a route that closely paralleled the tracks of the Missouri Pacific. Still unable to extend its line through the Indian Territory, the Frisco gave up its goal of constructing a transcontinental railroad to San Francisco and consolidated the western reaches of its system into their final form.

Further expansion of the Frisco system was halted in the late 1880s, and the road was swept into bankruptcy along with the Santa Fe in the mid-nineties. In 1896, the Frisco was reorganized as the St. Louis & San Francisco Railroad Company, with General B. F. Yoakum as general manager. He was later president and chairman during his long career with the company. Under Yoakum's direction, the Frisco doubled in size and changed its goal from the West Coast to the South. His aspiration was to a system that would span the mid-continent from the Twin Cities to the Gulf of Mexico.

The Frisco's prosperity was evidenced in 1906, when the railroad erected a new 13-story headquarters office building at the southwest corner of Ninth and Olive streets in downtown St. Louis. In 1917 the Frisco joined with the Katy to introduce the famous *Texas Special* offering deluxe service from St. Louis to San Antonio.

A 14-year period of reorganization was completed in 1947. Still using the same official name, the railroad's directors chose Clark Hungerford as the Frisco's new president, and another period of rebuilding began. One of the first moves was the introduction of new streamlined versions of the *Texas Special* and *Meteor* passenger trains powered by diesel locomotives in 1947. The former operated between St. Louis and San Antonio via Dallas–Fort Worth, while the latter train linked St. Louis with Oklahoma City via Tulsa. Hungerford was succeeded as president in 1962 by Lewis W. Menk, who relocated most of the Frisco offices from St. Louis to Springfield, Missouri, and also consolidated all train dispatching there.

Passenger service on the Frisco, which had been declining, was sharply reduced in September 1965, and ended completely on December 8, 1967, when the last train completed its run between Kansas City and Birmingham. This era culminated in 1977 with a joint application to the Interstate Commerce Commission for merger of the Frisco with the Burlington Northern Railroad.

After a temporary stay order to investigate a claim by the Katy that the merger would cause it damage, the Frisco became a part of the Burlington Northern Railroad on November 21, 1980. Locally, the merger meant the disappearance of a major railroad that had had its headquarters in St. Louis since the mid-nineteenth century. While an office was still maintained here, the Frisco Building at 906 Olive Street was sold and was renovated in a $12 million program by its new owners.

As part of the consolidation program by the Burlington after the merger, its freight yards in North St. Louis were absorbed by Frisco's large yards in the southwestern part of the city. With the abandonment of passenger service in the 1960s, all of the Frisco passenger stations were closed or sold, including its once-busy Tower Grove Station. That station was the hub of Frisco's commuter trains for many years, when there were stations at many points in St. Louis and its suburbs for trains operating between Union Station and Valley Park. According to a 1903 timetable, five trains ran in each direction Monday through Friday, fewer on weekends. Records indicate that such commuter service had been abandoned by 1924.

It was the construction of the St. Louis–San Francisco Railway through southwestern St. Louis in the 1880s that brought about the development of Lindenwood and Harlem Place. Although it never reached San Francisco, the Frisco was an important partner in the growth of St. Louis.

Ray Gehl

The Frisco's *Sunnyland* poses for a portrait with the men who accompanied her to Memphis during the 1950s.

The Katy *Flyer*, a "pioneer train," retired to the St. Louis Museum of Transport after an honorable career of opening the American West.

# MISSOURI, KANSAS & TEXAS RAILROAD— THE "KATY" LINES

While most of the Western railroad activity during the 1850s concentrated upon reaching the Pacific Coast, the idea of a railroad spanning the frontier from north to south was first proposed in the Kansas Territory during its fratricidal strife before the Civil War. Surveys of the route assured both Missouri and Kansas that the major part of the southwestern trade would flow through their gateways. Construction of the railway was considered essential for the growth of communities, for the taming of the land and its occupants, and for commercial and industrial development.

Originally chartered as the Union Pacific Railway Southern Branch, the Katy Railroad was born at a meeting of prominent Kansans in Emporia on September 20, 1865, with the idea for a line from Texas through Oklahoma, Kansas, and Missouri to St. Louis and Chicago. At another meeting in Emporia in February 1870, the railroad's new name was announced as the Missouri, Kansas & Texas Railway, soon popularly known as the "Katy."

Soon after reaching Denison, Texas, the Katy track crews turned their attention to the Northeastern Extension of the line beyond Sedalia. On May 31, 1873, the end of track reached Boonville on the Missouri River. Meanwhile, the track layers began on the northern side of the river and crews working south from Moberly met those coming north at Fayette, Missouri, on June 20, 1873. On July 4, a big celebration was held at Boonville, marking the completion of the line to Moberly, even though the bridge across the Missouri was unfinished.

The first train ran across the completed bridge, with its 363-foot drawspan, on January 10, 1874. Beyond Moberly, the Katy's next goal was Hannibal, Missouri, on the Mississippi River. A connection there was accomplished by acquisition of the Hannibal & Central Missouri Railroad, which had been under lease to the Toledo, Wabash & Western, a predecessor of the Wabash Railway. After reaching Hannibal and negotiating a connection with the Chicago, Burlington & Quincy Railroad, manager Robert S. Stevens proudly announced the introduction of Pullman Palace Sleeping Cars on trains from Chicago to Denison, Texas.

This began to cause apprehension in St. Louis, where the Board of Trade was asking if the Katy intended to bypass St. Louis. To counteract that sentiment, the Katy opened a St. Louis office in the Southern Hotel building, with Thomas Dorwin as general passenger agent. Stevens, as general manager, announced his desires that St. Louis be known as the natural outlet for the Katy and that the bulk of the line's traffic go through the St. Louis gateway. But he wanted it made clear that none of it should be routed via Vinita, Oklahoma, on his old rival, the Atlantic & Pacific Railway (later the Frisco). Therefore, Katy advertising emphasized that through trains would run on the Katy via Sedalia. This St. Louis connection was made over tracks of the Burlington and the Wabash.

Entry into St. Louis, mostly on its own trackage, was made possible by Katy's acquisition of the Missouri, Kansas & Eastern Railroad, built by St. Louis interests to tap the Katy's Sedalia railhead. Its bonds were guaranteed by the Katy, which finally acquired ownership in 1896. This St. Louis division was opened to traffic as far east as St. Charles in July 1893, but actual entry into St. Louis on Burlington trackage was delayed until that line finished its bridge across the Missouri River at Bellefontaine. The construction of Katy's terminals and connections with the new St. Louis Union Station were completed on March 16, 1895, marking the inauguration of through Katy passenger service from St. Louis. An interesting sidelight on the construction of the MK&E was the synthetic name chosen for one of its division points: Mokane, Missouri.

During the nineties, while engaged in a drive to recover from the Depression of 1893, and suffering increasing competition from its rivals, the Katy management decided that it needed some publicity. Its new general passenger agent, William Crush, who had a background as a promoter, devised the idea of the "Great Train Wreck." In this nation-

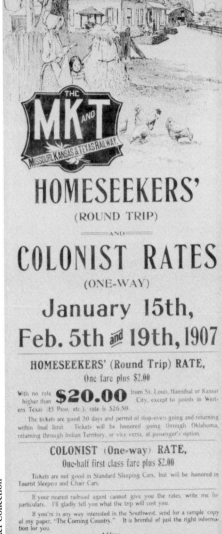

**A one-way ticket was all a determined homesteader needed. This 1907 Katy handbill shows the sylvan communities waiting out west.**

ally advertised stunt, two trains running in opposite directions on a
single track were to crash into each other head on. It took place on September 15, 1896, a few miles north of Waco, Texas. About 50,000 people assembled to witness the spectacle. The two trains crashed as
expected, but then an unforeseen thing happened: the boilers of the
locomotives exploded. Pieces of heavy metal wreckage rained down
upon the spectators, causing death and injury. Crush was immediately
fired, but was reinstated in his job the following day.

On January 1, 1918, during World War I, the nation's railroads
came under federal control. The Katy returned to receivership in
February 1920, having suffered from inept government control. A reorganization committee was soon busy, and as a result 476 miles of track
was removed from the system.

St. Louis lost the distinction of being the headquarters city of the
Katy in March 1957. Under its new president, William N. Deramus III of
Chicago, the Katy vacated its offices on the fifteenth floor of the Railway
Exchange Building, its address for many years, and moved its furniture
and records to Denison, Texas. The move was made clandestinely, on a
Sunday. When the office employees arrived for work on Monday
morning, they were greeted by empty offices. A notice stated that those
who wished to move to Texas should report there on Wednesday morning. St. Louisans were outraged when it was reported that Deramus had
no further comment. His attitude was compared to that of William H.
Vanderbilt, who, when asked if he intended to consult the public, once
replied "The public be damned."

Presently, the headquarters of the railroad that once ran the
famous *Bluebonnet* and *Katy Flyer* are in Dallas, Texas. A proposed
merger between the Katy and the Union Pacific Railroad was announced
in May 1985, but was called off in August.

# St. Louis Southwestern Railway Lines— The Cotton Belt Route

Two rather diverse desires led to the eventual birth of the St. Louis Southwestern Railway Lines, now popularly known as the Cotton Belt Route.

First of these was the determination of the citizens of Tyler, Texas, to connect their town with a major railroad. In 1877, they began construction of a 21½-mile narrow-gauge railroad with the unusual name of Tyler Tap Railroad. By 1879, the Tyler group ran into financial trouble. Their venture was rescued by some St. Louis cotton merchants headed by James W. Paramore, who foresaw the need for direct rail access from St. Louis to the cotton fields of eastern Texas. These two interests combined their efforts and formed the Texas & St. Louis Railway Company, which extended its trackage southwestward to Waco, Texas, by September 1881. Toward St. Louis, their plans called for a line to Texarkana, Arkansas, where a direct connection to St. Louis could be achieved over the tracks of the St. Louis & Iron Mountain Railroad. However, the new line's backers met opposition from Jay Gould, who had recently added the Iron Mountain line to his southwestern railroad empire. Gould's purpose was to force the fledgling railroad to give up or sell out.

Paramore refused to be bullied by Gould; he decided to build his own line through Arkansas and Missouri to Cairo, Illinois. This was done by another new company called the Texas & St. Louis Railway

Company of Arkansas and Missouri. Through new construction and connections with other railroads, Paramore's system had a 752-mile rail line from Gatesville, Texas, to Bird's Point, Missouri, on the Mississippi River opposite Cairo. By this time, the line had acquired its popular name, the Cotton Belt Route, and the final connection to St. Louis was made from Cairo through Illinois to East St. Louis over the tracks of the St. Louis & Cairo Railroad, popularly known as the Cairo Short Line. This agreement was reached on May 29, 1882. In Missouri, an important branch line was built from New Madrid to Malden, in the rich southeastern Missouri cotton country.

During the 1880s the line continued to rely upon its narrow-gauge rails, which Paramore believed efficient for the transportation of a lightweight commodity such as cotton. In 1882, Paramore built a $200,000 cotton compress in East St. Louis to handle the staple brought there by the Cotton Belt.

The Cotton Belt first reached St. Louis through Missouri in 1901 over track of the Missouri Pacific, but in 1905 it shifted to the Illinois side of the river, using Mo Pac's east side line from Thebes, Illinois. Earlier, the Cotton Belt had adopted standard-gauge track width to make it compatible with connecting lines.

For a brief time in 1925, the Cotton Belt was controlled by the Rock Island, but its management soon passed to the Kansas City Southern. Since 1932, the Cotton Belt has been under control of the Southern Pacific. Between 1935 and 1947, the Cotton Belt again experienced financial difficulties, but in this instance it survived without distributing the stock equity, an unusual occurrence in the experience of bankrupt railroads.

Passenger traffic on the Cotton Belt was much subordinated to its freight carriers, with freight revenue accounting for about 100 times its passenger revenue in 1951. Its principal passenger trains were the *Lone Star* and the *Morning Star* between St. Louis and Dallas–Fort Worth. They were sometimes sidetracked to allow a fast freight train to pass. The last passenger runs on the Cotton Belt were made in December 1959.

After having its headquarters in St. Louis for a great many years, the Cotton Belt moved its administrative offices to Tyler, Texas, in 1954. It was the first of the six railroads that at various times relocated their head offices out of St. Louis. Since 1930, the Cotton Belt offices had been in the building on the west side of Fourth Street between Pine and Chestnut that was once home of the Planters Hotel, which closed in 1922. This was a ten-story Victorian structure, built in 1893, that became known as the Cotton Belt Building after the railroad became its principal tenant. After being vacated by the Cotton Belt, the building served a declining number of tenants until it was razed in 1972 to make way for the new Boatmen's Bank Tower.

Presently, the Cotton Belt System operates about 1,500 miles of track southwest from St. Louis to Texas, with offshoots in Illinois, Tennessee, and Louisiana.

The line officially adopted the name St. Louis Southwestern Railway in 1891.

Donald A. Sarno Collection

**The Cotton Belt Route capitalized on its Texas connection with the *Lone Star* trains.**

A popular train on a popular route, the *City of Kansas City* was a steady moneymaker for the Wabash line.

# THE NORTH MISSOURI RAILROAD AND THE WABASH

For a railroad that would operate lines east and west from St. Louis, the origin of the Wabash System occurred in two widespread locations.

Its line from St. Louis to Kansas City and northern Missouri began as the North Missouri Railroad, incorporated on March 3, 1851. This railroad was to be built from St. Charles, Missouri, to the Iowa state line, and thence to Ottumwa and Chariton, Iowa. Its charter was amended in 1852 to permit an extension from St. Charles to St. Louis.

Construction began in May 1854 and reached the Missouri River opposite St. Charles on August 2, 1855. Building westward through Warrenton and Mexico, the line reached Moberly late in 1858 and Macon, Missouri, in February 1859, just before the outbreak of the Civil War.

State aid secured in 1865 enabled the North Missouri Railroad to reach Kansas City in 1869 and to build a northern extension to the Iowa line and a bridge at St. Charles. The bridge was opened in 1871, but required rebuilding after span collapses in 1879 and 1881. It was replaced by the present bridge in 1936.

After foreclosure, the North Missouri Railroad was assigned to the St. Louis, Kansas City & Northern Railway in 1872. A line from Ferguson, Missouri, into St. Louis was opened in 1876. On February 2, 1878, the first through train to St. Paul departed from the St. Louis Union Depot. Originally the entry into St. Louis by the North Missouri Railroad was along the riverfront from the north, with a depot at North Market Street. The line from Ferguson came into the city from the northwest through a corner of Forest Park and thence to a link-up with tracks into the Union Depot at Twelfth and Poplar streets.

The St. Louis, Kansas City & Northern was absorbed by the Wabash Railway Company in 1879. Popularly known as the Wabash, it established its headquarters in St. Louis in 1880. In 1870, the Wabash had acquired the Decatur & East St. Louis Railroad for an entry into St. Louis from the east.

Accommodation trains began running between the east bank of the Missouri River opposite St. Charles and St. Louis in 1855. Two trains operated daily in each direction carrying freight and passengers on weekdays and passengers only on Sundays. As the area through which they ran became more populated, the trains carried considerable commuter traffic. A regular daily train, popularly known to its commuter patrons as "The Comm," originated in St. Charles each morning and returned each evening. Ferguson became its major stop, and considerable rivalry developed between Ferguson riders and those from St. Charles. There were 18 stops for the train before it reached its St. Louis terminus on the elevated tracks at Eads Bridge Station. The Comm continued to operate until 1933.

Ferguson Station was so named by the North Missouri Railroad in honor of the town's founder, who donated a right-of-way along the western edge of his property. In later years, the Wabash opened a recreational club for its employees in Ferguson. Known as the Wabash Club, its grounds are now a city park. The lake in the park was a source of water for locomotives during the steam engine era.

A convenience for St. Louis patrons was the Wabash Delmar Station at Delmar Boulevard and Hodiamont Avenue in the West End. This handsome limestone structure with a marble interior opened in 1929, replacing an earlier wooden depot. Passengers could board trains there for Chicago or Kansas City. Falling into disuse with the decline of railroad passenger traffic, the station was closed in 1970. It was suggested for various uses, such as a commuter station on a rapid transit system, but when these ideas failed the building was slated for demolition. However, in June 1983 it was sold and restored by a lighting company for its offices.

By 1947, with Norman B. Pitcairn as its president, the Wabash System had 2,393 miles of trackage, and operated such well-known passenger trains as the *Banner Blue Limited,* the *Blue Bird* to Chicago, and the streamliner *City of St. Louis* to Kansas City. A popular train to Detroit for many years was the Wabash *Cannonball.*

All Wabash trains had their fans, and one, the Wabash
*Cannonball*, even had its own song.

Upgrading its passenger service in the 1950s, the Wabash was proud of its new $1.5 million *Blue Bird* dome car train between St. Louis and Chicago. Its coach passengers enjoyed amenities usually reserved for extra-fare riders, such as a club car with a coffee bar and lounge chairs. Operation of streamlined trains began on the Wabash in 1946, allowing through coach and Pullman service to the West Coast. Their second streamliner, the *City of Kansas City*, was inaugurated by General Omar Bradley, who had been a Wabash employee in his youth.

A major change came to the Wabash in 1964, when it was absorbed by the Norfolk & Western, along with the Nickel Plate and two smaller railroads. At the time, it was the largest rail merger in history. In the process, St. Louis lost the Wabash headquarters office (in the Railway Exchange Building) to Roanoke, Virginia.

The Norfolk & Western Railway combined with the Southern Railway on June 1, 1982, to form the Norfolk Southern Railway Corporation. At that time, this great rail system was the fourth largest in the nation, with 18,000 miles of track network operating in 21 states.

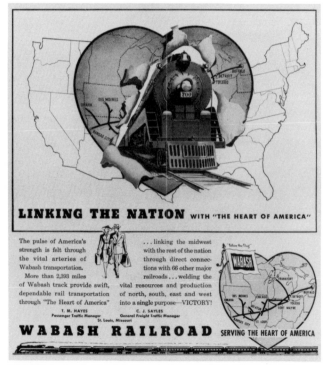

This Wabash ad, combining sentimentality and patriotism,
urged America to take it to heart during World War II.

# St. Louis, Kansas City & Colorado Railroad and the Rock Island

One of the earliest midwestern railroads, the Chicago, Rock Island & Pacific, was popularly known as the Rock Island Lines. It was organized on February 27, 1847, with the purpose of linking Rock Island, Illinois, on the Mississippi River with barge traffic on the Illinois River. The Rock Island had the distinction of being the first railroad to reach the Mississippi and the first to cross it by bridge.

In a lawsuit with steamboat interests, the railroad was once represented by Abraham Lincoln. Two weeks after the bridge was opened in 1856, the packet steamboat *Effie Afton* drifted into the bridge and caught fire. The blaze destroyed the boat and part of the bridge. The trial produced an order to remove the bridge, but after an appeal to the U.S. Supreme Court, the right to span navigable streams was upheld in 1862.

On June 21, 1873, the Rock Island fell victim to the first holdup of a moving train in the West. This was an attack by the Jesse James gang at Adair, Iowa. They escaped with $3,000; a $75,000 gold shipment eluded them because it had been shipped the day before.

The Rock Island's story in the St. Louis area began in 1872 with the organization of the proposed St. Louis County Railroad. It was the idea of Jonathan Jones, founder of the Jones Commercial College in St. Louis. Several wealthy St. Louisans subscribed $40,000 in conditional stock and elected Jones as the company president. They chose W. Mark Kasson of New York to develop the project. After a survey was made, most of the right-of-way was donated. Work began at a point on Old Bonhomme Road, but was stopped as soon as 55 percent of the stock and $25,000 of first mortgage bonds were issued. In 1874, the portion of the right-of-way from downtown to Union Avenue was sold to the Wabash Railroad for $125,000. During the ensuing years the project had eight different names as it was sold and resold.

Finally, in the early 1880s it was reorganized as the St. Louis, Kansas City & Colorado Railroad, and by 1884 construction of the line was under way eastward from Clayton to Forsyth Junction, near DeBaliviere Avenue, where its tracks crossed those of the Wabash. Operations began on March 6, 1887, when the company began running two trains in each direction daily between St. Louis and Creve Coeur, using the Wabash tracks into the Union Depot at Twelfth and Poplar streets.

In 1893, the railroad was sold to the Santa Fe; it was sold again in 1901 to the Rock Island, which completed it as far west as Union, Missouri. However, the irregular rail service proved unsatisfactory to the citizens of Clayton, who had excellent electric trolley car service. In 1917, the Rock Island discontinued its passenger trains through Clayton and announced that it would enter St. Louis on the Wabash tracks.

In 1925, after real estate development near its Clayton depot, the Rock Island resumed passenger service. This was soon discontinued, and when the Wabash tracks were placed into an open-cut at DeBaliviere Avenue in 1935, the Rock Island tracks west from Forsyth Junction became isolated and virtually unused.

On December 27, 1950, the Missouri Public Service Commission authorized the abandonment of the Rock Island tracks in St. Louis and Clayton. Through service to Kansas City was routed over the tracks of the Missouri Pacific Railroad. In the meantime, the Rock Island had built its own line to Kansas City via Union, Eldon, Versailles, and Pleasant Hill. This was used for local service only, until the demise of the Rock Island Lines.

The former right-of-way of the Rock Island from DeBaliviere Avenue westward through University City and Clayton is now the route of the Forest Park Expressway and Millbrook Boulevard.

# ST. LOUIS, KEOKUK & NORTHWESTERN RAILROAD AND THE BURLINGTON

On February 14, 1855, three Illinois railroads officially joined together under the name of Chicago, Burlington & Quincy Railroad. The names represented the three terminals of their lines, after completion of the branch from Galesburg to Quincy on January 31, 1856. A direct line from Aurora to Chicago was opened for service in 1864.

Plans were laid by an independent company to build a railroad from Rock Island south to the Burlington main line at Monmouth and thence to East St. Louis. After a long delay, the project known as the Rockford, Rock Island & St. Louis Railroad was completed in 1867. In February 1877 it came under Burlington control, which gave it an entrance into the St. Louis district. Another approach to St. Louis was begun in the late 1870s with the construction of the St. Louis, Keokuk & Northwestern Railroad along the west bank of the Mississippi as far south as Old Monroe, Missouri. This railroad was acquired by the Burlington during the 1880s, but an actual entrance by the CB&Q into St. Louis on this route was not achieved until the completion of a southward extension and a bridge across the Missouri River at Bellefontaine, Missouri, in 1894.

Trackage for the Burlington's St. Louis, Keokuk & Northwestern Railroad branch into St. Louis was built in 1888-89 when its freight yard was established at Second Street and Franklin Avenue. The Keokuk route, also known as the St. Louis, Minneapolis and St. Paul Short Line, had access to St. Louis at that time through the Union Bridge and Terminal Company. When the new St. Louis Union Station opened in 1894, the first train to depart was the Burlington "Fast Mail."

In 1898, the Burlington System embraced 56 different lines with 5,730 miles of track. On April 17, 1901, it came under the control of James J. Hill and his financial agent, J. P. Morgan, and in the next year it became a member of the St. Louis Terminal Railroad Association.

By 1940, the Burlington System operated more than 11,000 miles of track in 14 states. The road had become a pioneer in streamlined passenger trains with the introduction of the Burlington *Zephyr* in 1934. This first diesel-electric streamline train in Amercia began service on November 11, 1934, as the *Pioneer Zephyr* between Omaha and Kansas City. The merger of the Burlington with the Northern Pacific and Great Northern railroads to form the 25,000-mile Burlington-Northern System tem occurred in 1970, and on November 21, 1980, it acquired control of the St. Louis & San Francisco (Frisco) Railway.

## BURLINGTON'S STREAMLINE FLEET

### DIESEL POWERED • • • BUILT OF STAINLESS STEEL

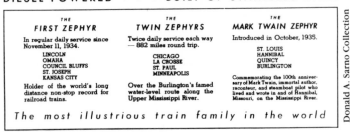

| THE FIRST ZEPHYR | THE TWIN ZEPHYRS | THE MARK TWAIN ZEPHYR | |
|---|---|---|---|
| In regular daily service since November 11, 1934. | Twice daily service each way — 882 miles round trip. | Introduced in October, 1935. | Donald A. Sarno Collection |
| LINCOLN OMAHA COUNCIL BLUFFS ST. JOSEPH KANSAS CITY | CHICAGO LA CROSSE ST. PAUL MINNEAPOLIS | ST. LOUIS HANNIBAL QUINCY BURLINGTON | |
| Holder of the world's long distance non-stop record for railroad trains. | Over the Burlington's famed water-level route along the Upper Mississippi River. | Commemorating the 100th anniversary of Mark Twain, immortal author, raconteur, and steamboat pilot who lived and wrote in and of Hannibal, Missouri, on the Mississippi River. | |
| *The most illustrious train family in the world* | | | |

Speed and smoothness marked the routes of the Zephyr trains.

# THE CHICAGO & ALTON RAILROAD

The first of several railroads to connect St. Louis with Chicago was the Chicago & Alton, which had its beginning with the Alton & Sangamon Railroad. It was chartered in 1847, commenced in 1849, and completed between Alton and Springfield in 1852. It was extended to Bloomington in 1854 and to Joliet in 1855 by the Chicago & Mississippi Railroad, chartered on February 27, 1847.

It was thought advisable to have a rail connection between the growing river port of Alton and the state capital at Springfield, but an extension to a point opposite St. Louis would have been contrary to Illinois state policy, which forbade any public measure facilitating the transfer of business to cities of other states. Connection with St. Louis from Alton was by packet line steamboats. Entry into Chicago from Joliet was made over tracks of the Rock Island Railroad. On February 16, 1861, the company was reorganized as the Chicago & Alton Railroad.

Until 1861, passengers for St. Louis were carried there from Alton by steamboat packets on the Mississippi River. The steamers *Winchester* and *Reindeer* were used in this service. It was announced that these boats were equipped with washrooms and baths, affording passengers an opportunity to arrive in St. Louis clean and refreshed after the long railroad ride, which took 15½ hours overall.

In 1864 an offer to merge the newly completed and independent Alton & St. Louis Railroad was accepted by the Chicago & Alton. In the

The Alton ("The Only Way") had reason to boast: it introduced the nation's first dining car and first sleeper.

years between 1861 and 1864, St. Louis–bound passengers were transported to East St. Louis by arrangements with the Terre Haute & Alton Railroad, which later became a part of the New York Central System.

A unique liaison in railroad history was the association of the Chicago & Alton with George M. Pullman in the early development of sleeping and dining cars. In 1858, Pullman, a cabinetmaker, approached management with his idea of converting day coaches into sleeping cars for use on long overnight railroad trips. The railroad gave Pullman three cars to experiment with at his own expense. When these cars proved to be successful after 1859, Pullman completed the *Pioneer* in 1865 as the first railroad car built especially for use as a "sleeper" at the then staggering cost of $20,000. This car was attached to the funeral train of Abraham Lincoln at the request of Mrs. Lincoln. As the Chicago & Alton was the route for the funeral train from Chicago to Springfield, the railroad was required to conduct hurried improvements to its bridges and trackage facilities along the line.

Pullman founded the Pullman Palace Car Company in 1867, and in the next year he built the first dining car, called the *Delmonico*. The use of this car by the Alton gave the railroad the claim to fame as the first rail line in the world to operate a "diner." By the turn of the century, the Chicago & Alton Railroad, popularly called the "Alton," was a compact system operating on both sides of the Mississippi, in the states of Illinois and Missouri, with Chicago, St. Louis, and Kansas City as its principal terminals. Its direct routes earned for the Alton the distinction of its slogan: "C&A—the Only Way."

On September 28, 1924, the Chicago & Alton introduced the new *Alton Limited*, the "Handsomest Train in the World," for service between Chicago and St. Louis. This deluxe train covered the distance between the two cities in the fast time of six and one-half hours.

In 1946, the financially ailing Chicago & Alton was acquired by the Gulf, Mobile & Ohio Railroad in a merger. The Alton Route's principal trains continued in operation, including the *Alton Limited, Abraham Lincoln,* and *Ann Rutledge,* By that time, these trains had a running time of five hours and ten minutes between Chicago and St. Louis.

Like most other American railroads, the Alton discontinued its passenger service when Amtrak was established in 1971. The former Chicago & Alton trackage became a part of the Illinois Central Gulf System in 1972 when the Gulf, Mobile & Ohio merged with the Illinois Central.

# THE ILLINOIS CENTRAL RAILROAD AND ITS ST. LOUIS CONNECTIONS

An early rail approach to St. Louis from southern Illinois was a joint operation of the St. Louis, Alton & Terre Haute Railroad and the Illinois Central. The line from East St. Louis to the DuQuoin, Illinois, junction with the Illinois Central was originally a part of the St. Louis, Alton & Terre Haute, whose predecessor lines dated back to 1851. This line and one from East St. Louis to Belleville were opened in the mid-1850s. This company was reorganized as the St. Louis, Alton & Terre Haute in 1861.

A line from Belleville to a junction with the Illinois Central at DuQuoin was completed in 1873. In 1895 the IC assumed operation of the trackage to DuQuoin, giving the Illinois Central direct entry into St. Louis. Another entry into St. Louis by the IC was on a line from Springfield southward through Mount Olive and Glen Carbon. This 97-mile line to East St. Louis was the result of the consolidation of several companies, and was finally achieved in 1895. By 1899 this line was bankrupt; the Springfield to East St. Louis portion was purchased by E. H. Harriman and conveyed to the Illinois Central in exchange for $3 million in IC bonds.

On June 17, 1900, the deluxe passenger trains *Diamond Special* and *Daylight Special* began operating on this line between Chicago and St. Louis. The Illinois Central sought for many years to improve its business connections with St. Louis. An early member of its directorate was Pierre Chouteau, Jr., a nephew of one of the city's founders, who was prominent in the fur trade. His prophecy that the Illinois Central would eventually extend its tracks into St. Louis was finally realized.

Events on the night of April 29, 1910, gave the Illinois Central some undesired fame through the southbound *Cannon Ball* with Casey Jones at the throttle. Speeding along at 70 miles an hour, Casey learned too late that three cars of a sidetracked freight were still on the main line. Despite Casey's heroic efforts, he could not slow his train in time, and in the resulting crash he was killed when the locomotive overturned. Casey, who had not deserted his post as engineer even in the face of certain death, became a legend of bravery among railroad men.

By the mid-1950s the Illinois Central was operating 6,582 miles of first main track. Its luxury passenger train was the *Panama Limited*. This crack train between Chicago and New Orleans was placed in service on December 2, 1934, on an 18-hour schedule between its terminals, two hours faster than any previous train on that route. Other well-known fast trains on the IC were the *Green Diamond* and the *City of Miami*.

In 1972, the Illinois Central and the Gulf, Mobile & Ohio railroads were merged to form the present 9,600-mile Illinois Central Gulf Railroad System.

Donald A. Sarno Collection

The sleek art deco logo of the *Green Diamond* welcomed travelers to modern service on the St. Louis to Chicago run.

# CHICAGO & EASTERN ILLINOIS RAILROAD

Although it began in the early 1870s as the Chicago, Danville & Vincennes Railroad, connecting those three cities, the Chicago & Eastern Illinois Railroad began using its modern name in the late 1880s. During the 1890s, the C&EI extended branches to Evansville, Indiana, and also southward through Illinois, from Shelbyville through Salem to Joppa on the Ohio River and to Thebes on the Mississippi.

Entry of the Chicago & Eastern Illinois Railroad into St. Louis was achieved in advance of the St. Louis World's Fair of 1904. Its access was by an arrangement to use the tracks of the Big Four Railroad from Pana, Illinois, via Hillsboro, Livingston, Mitchell, and Granite City into St. Louis Union Station. Its system included 1,276 miles of track by 1915.

During the 1930s, the C&EI operated two deluxe air-conditioned trains between St. Louis and Chicago. The daylight train, the *Century of Progress*, ran on a fast five-hour schedule; the midnight train, the *Spirit of Progress*, featured a radio-equipped cafe-lounge car and valet service.

By the 1960s the Chicago & Eastern Illinois Railroad had fallen upon economic hard times. In June 1969, its Evansville branch was sold to the Louisville & Nashville Railroad. The remaining portion of the C&EI was merged with the Missouri Pacific Railroad on October 17, 1976. It is now part of the Union Pacific System.

# THE OHIO & MISSISSIPPI RAILROAD AND THE BALTIMORE & OHIO

First of the railroads from the eastern states to reach the St. Louis area was the Ohio & Mississippi, which received its initial charter in Indiana on February 14, 1848. This charter provided for the construction of a railroad across the state from Lawrenceburg to Vincennes, with connections to Cincinnati and to Illinoistown, opposite St. Louis on the Mississippi River. The franchise was soon approved by Ohio, but difficulty was encountered in Illinois, which would not approve it unless the line terminated at Alton, helping that city to become a formidable commerical rival of St. Louis.

Prominent citizens eventually succeeded in convincing the Illinois legislature to grant the charter early in 1851. The Ohio & Mississippi Railroad Company of Illinois was incorporated on February 12, 1851, to build a line from Illinoistown to the state line near Vincennes, Indiana. In St. Louis, an Ohio & Mississippi Railroad mass meeting was held in the rotunda of the Old Courthouse on March 28, 1849, to consider a plan to loan $500,000 of the city's credit to the proposed railroad. This resulted in an election which returned a large majority in favor of the plan.

Groundbreaking ceremonies were held at Illinoistown on February 7, 1852, and the last spike completing the line to Cincinnati was driven on August 15, 1857, near Mitchell, Indiana. This occasion was celebrated in St. Louis by a parade and jubilant civic ceremonies.

The track gauge of the O&M was changed in 1871 from six feet to four feet eight inches to conform to the standard gauge of the Baltimore & Ohio and the Marietta & Cincinnati railroads, with which it connected at Cincinnati.

This railroad was a contributing factor in the growth of Illinoistown, now called East St. Louis. Its machine shops were built there on a four-acre, manmade elevated plateau about a mile from the Mississippi River.

In 1871, the Ohio & Mississippi, along with other railroads operating in the St. Louis area, formed the Union Depot Company to facilitate the transfer of passengers. It opened the Union Depot at Twelfth and Poplar streets after the completion of the Eads Bridge and tunnel in 1874. A similar organization was effected in 1889 in conjunction with plans for the new Union Station at Eighteenth and Market streets. The O&M was one of the original members of the Terminal Railroad Association of St. Louis.

On November 1, 1893, the Ohio & Mississippi Railroad was consolidated with the Baltimore & Ohio Railroad as the Baltimore & Ohio Southwestern Railroad Company, giving St. Louis a direct connection through Cincinnati to Baltimore and Washington, D.C., on the Atlantic seaboard. The B&O was organized in Baltimore in 1827. During the heyday of railroad passenger traffic the Baltimore & Ohio operated such luxury trains as the all-Pullman *Capitol Limited* from Chicago and the *National Limited* from St. Louis to Washington. Passenger service on the B&O was discontinued with the advent of Amtrak in 1971.

In 1973 the Baltimore & Ohio, the Chesapeake & Ohio, and the Western Maryland railroads combined as separate entities under a holding company known as the Chessie System. In 1979 the Chessie System, Inc., and the Family Lines combined to form the CSX Corporation System.

"Solid vestibuled" trains, touted in the *World's Fair Bulletin* as the very latest thing, allowed passengers to move from car to car without stepping outdoors.

# THE "BEE LINE," THE "BIG FOUR," AND THE NEW YORK CENTRAL SYSTEM

An early railroad link between St. Louis and Indianapolis was the Indianapolis & St. Louis Railroad, chartered on August 31, 1867, and opened on July 1, 1870.

It later became a part of the "Bee Line," which connected with the former Bellefontaine & Indiana Railroad. It was called the Bee Line because much of its activity was centered in Bellefontaine, Ohio. On its route from Terre Haute to St. Louis, the Bee Line ran through Pana, Mattoon, and Granite City in Illinois.

In 1889, the Bee Line, along with two other railroads, was consolidated into the Cleveland, Cincinnati, Chicago & St. Louis Railroad, soon known as the "Big Four." In 1930 the Big Four, controlled through stock ownership by the New York Central, was leased by its owning company for 99 years. By 1950, the Big Four operated a total of 4,968 miles of track.

The New York Central Railroad, which operated the *Southwestern Limited* between St. Louis and New York, and the crack *Twentieth Century Limited* from Chicago, was one of America's first railroads. Its career began in 1831, when service was begun on the 17-mile Mohawk & Hudson Railroad between Albany and Schenectady, New York.

Its first train was pulled by a small locomotive, the *De Witt Clinton*, hauling several cars converted from stagecoaches. By 1836, the iron horse was making daily 78-mile trips between Schenectady and Utica, and seven years later it was possible to go all the way to Buffalo, a distance of 399 miles. However, several car changes were necessary en route and the whole journey took almost 24 hours. This was the beginning of the New York Central Railroad, incorporated under that name in 1853.

During the latter part of the nineteenth century, under the able management of the Vanderbilt interests, the New York Central became one of the dominant railroads in the eastern United States. An epic event in the history of the New York Central occurred on May 10, 1893, when the great new locomotive No. 999 pulled the *Empire State Express* at the incredible speed of 112½ miles an hour on a 36-mile run from Batavia, New York, to Buffalo.

Also during 1893, the new *Exposition Flyer* made the 969-mile run from New York to Chicago in just 18 hours. It proved to be a worthy predecessor of the *Twentieth Century Limited,* the Central's all-time deluxe train, which began service on June 15, 1902. In 1905 the *Century's* running time was reduced from 20 hours to 18 hours. By 1935, the running time was further reduced to 16½ hours. On June 15, 1938, a brand-new *Twentieth Century Limited,* pulled by a new streamlined version of the Hudson locomotive, began the run to Chicago on a 16-hour schedule.

From the first, the New York Central sought to run its lines through river valleys and along the lake shores, where grades were slight and trains could travel fast and ride easy. The Central adopted the slogan "The Water Level Route." Its system included 11,000 miles of first-line track, including such subsidiaries as the Big Four, the Michigan Central, the West Shore, and the Boston & Albany.

In 1968, the New York Central merged with its rival, the Pennsylvania Railroad, to form the Penn-Central Railroad, which went bankrupt in 1970. By 1973, the bankruptcy of virtually the entire northeastern rail network called for drastic governmental action. It came in the form of the Rail Reorganization Act, which established the United States Railroad Association to plan a rationalized network, and the Consolidated Rail Corporation, or Conrail, to administer the resulting system. It began operation with a $6 billion subsidy in 1976. But by the end of the decade it was asking for more government money to cope with perennial problems of dilapidated equipment and crippling overheads.

Conrail has since been turned around into a success story. It has grown into one of the most modern and efficient railroads in the nation. With 13,500 miles of track and an average of nearly 800 trains a day, it is one of the primary transport systems in the Northeast. Conrail's profits have risen from $39 million in 1981 to more than $500 million in 1984.

The *Detroit Arrow* (c. 1910) displays the Keystone logo that the Pennsylvania Railroad borrowed from the Keystone State.

# THE VANDALIA LINE
# AND THE PENNSYLVANIA RAILROAD

St. Louis commercial interests quite early recognized the desirability of a railroad connection with the Atlantic seaboard. A railroad along a line from St. Louis to Terre Haute and Indianapolis was projected in 1837 as part of a state-run railroad in Illinois that proved unsuccessful.

Ten years later, the Mississippi & Illinois Railroad was incorporated to construct a line from Illinoistown (East St. Louis) through Vandalia to Terre Haute, Indiana. A convention was held at Vandalia in 1850 to organize a company to build it. However, no real progress occurred until February 10, 1865, when the St. Louis, Vandalia & Terre Haute Railroad was chartered.

Later, the "Vandalia Line," aided by the Pennsylvania Railroad, progressed rapidly along its route across Illinois. It was opened from East St. Louis to Highland in 1868, to Effingham in 1869, and into Indianapolis in June 1870. In the same year, through service on the Vandalia from St. Louis to Chicago was effected via the Illinois Central.

In 1878, the Vandalia line was leased to interests including the Pittsburgh, Cincinnati & St. Louis Railroad, whose interest was guaranteed by the Pennsylvania. During the 1880s, the Vandalia line was reorganized as a part of the Pennsylvania System from St. Louis to New York.

By the 1890s, the Vandalia-Pennsylvania, as it was then called, claimed to be the first railroad in America to introduce block signals, automatic switches, and track tanks, as well as air brakes, limited trains, and complete dining car service. It called itself "The Standard Railroad of America."

The idea of a railroad across Pennsylvania originated in 1825 when Philadelphia commerical interests became uneasy about the opening of the Erie Canal in New York state. After various means of transport were used, including canals and portage railroads with inclined planes, an act to incorporate the Pennsylvania Railroad to Pittsburgh was approved by the state legislature in 1846. Its first train reached Pittsburgh in 1858. Eventual connection to St. Louis began in 1865 with the completion of a line to Columbus, Ohio; five years later East St. Louis was reached via the Vandalia line.

Most spectacular of the engineering achievements in the building of the Pennsylvania Railroad was the Horseshoe Curve. About five miles west of Altoona, in its climb to the summit of the mountain range, the main line doubles back across the Kitanning Valley, forming a great U turn. The rise to the 2,200-foot summit is 92 feet to the mile, or nearly a 1.8 percent grade. Thus, between the two ends of the U the tracks have climbed 122 feet. In reaching the summit at Gallitzin, the tracks have risen 1,015 feet in the 11 miles from Altoona.

In New York City the Pennsylvania Railroad's main line terminated in the great Pennsylvania Station. Designed in neoclassical style by Stanford White, it welcomed its first train in 1910. Perhaps the best known train using Penn Station was the *Broadway Limited*, the Pennsy's premier train to Chicago. Its predecessor, the *Pennsylvania Special*, made the fastest train run recorded in the United States, running three miles near Ada, Ohio, in 85 seconds on June 12, 1905, at an average speed of 127.06 miles per hour. This feat stood as the world record for nearly 50 years.

On November 24, 1912, the *Special*'s name was changed to the *Broadway Limited* (named not for the famous street in New York, but for the great broad way of steel of the Pennsylvania Railroad). Other famous Pennsylvania trains were the *Manhattan Limited*, the New York to Washington *Congressional Limited*, the *American* and the *Spirit of St. Louis* (named in honor of Lindbergh's plane on his flight to Paris in 1927).

With the drop in railroad passenger traffic after World War II, Pennsylvania Station in New York was demolished in 1963.

A surprising event in 1968 was the merger of two old rivals, the Pennsylvania and the New York Central, into the Penn-Central Railroad. Unfortunately, economic hard times found the new company running out of credit two years later. Under the 1973 Rail Reorganization Act, the United States Railroad Association was formed to plan a rationalized rail network in the northeastern United States. It was administered by the Consolidated Rail Corporation, or Conrail, which absorbed the Penn-Central.

An omen of darker days to come can be glimpsed in this sunny 1927 ad announcing the re-naming of the *St. Louisan* and the *New Yorker* for Lindbergh's *Spirit of St. Louis*. The shadow of passenger aviation would fall more heavily on the railroads by the early 1960s.

# TOLEDO, ST. LOUIS & WESTERN RAILROAD AND THE NICKEL PLATE

The St. Louis connection of the railroad that later became the "Nickel Plate Road" was operated under various names during its career. It was known as the Toledo, Delphos & Bloomington Railroad during its early years in Ohio and Indiana. It made its entry into East St. Louis in 1883, branching off from its main line at Delphos, Ohio, to form a direct route from Toledo to St. Louis. At that time, it was the longest narrow-gauge railroad east of the Mississippi, with about 910 miles of track. Its name then was the Toledo, Cincinnati & St. Louis Railroad, known as the "Clover Leaf Route" because of the trefoil symbol trademark on its cars. In 1887, its track gauge was converted to standard in order to connect properly with intersecting railroads. By then known as the Toledo, St. Louis & Western Railroad, it was to become the western division of the Nickel Plate Road in 1923.

The New York, Chicago & St. Louis Railroad, also known as the Nickel Plate Road, was projected by a syndicate that controlled the Lake Erie & Western Railroad, and was originally conceived in 1880 as an extension of that railroad. Original plans to build the line to St. Louis were abandoned; it was built between Buffalo and Chicago.

The line was completed in September 1882. The first regular passenger train was operated from Chicago on October 23, 1882. By then, the line was popularly known as the "Nickel Plate Road," a nickname coined by F. R. Loomis, editor of the Norwalk (Ohio) *Chronicle,* on

March 10, 1881, to describe the glittering prospects of the railroad.

The New York, Chicago & St. Louis Railroad was consolidated in 1923 from five railroads, including its namesake and the Toledo, St. Louis & Western, which gave the Nickel Plate a direct entry to St. Louis.

Control of the Nickel Plate passed to the Chesapeake & Ohio Railway on December 29, 1937, through acquisition of stock owned by the Allegheny Corporation. On November 10, 1947, C&O disposed of its Nickel Plate stock by distributing it as a dividend to C&O stockholders. At that time, in conjunction with the Delaware, Lackawanna & Western Railroad, the Nickel Plate operated the *Nickel Plate Limited* between New York and Chicago and the *Westerner* to St. Louis.

In 1964, the Nickel Plate was absorbed by the Norfolk & Western System, which became the Norfolk Southern in 1982, after a merger with the Southern Railway System.

Donald A. Sarno Collection

A *Nickel Plate* timetable of 1949 features St. Louis' Milles Fountain with Union Station as a stately backdrop.

® *"Sleep Like a Kitten"*

# CHESAPEAKE & OHIO RAILWAY

After the Civil War, the states of Virginia and West Virginia united to combine the Virginia Central and the Covington & Ohio railroads into the Chesapeake & Ohio Railroad Company in 1868.

Completion westward to Huntington, West Virginia, on the Ohio River was achieved in 1873. This city was surveyed in 1870 as the terminus of the C&O and was named for that railroad's principal "upbuilder," Collis P. Huntington. He was one of the group of four wealthy California merchants who built the Central Pacific and Southern Pacific railroads. Huntington visualized the C&O as the eastern link of his proposed transcontinental railroad.

In 1878, the C&O was sold under foreclosure and reorganized as the Chesapeake & Ohio Railway Company. In 1890 the Richmond & Allegheny Railway, operating through the James River Valley between Richmond and Clifton Forge, was acquired. The Chesapeake & Ohio established a pedigree with its purchase of the James River Company, incorporated in 1785 with George Washington as its first (though inactive) president. This gave the C&O the right to call itself "George Washington's Railroad."

During the 1890s the Big Four Railroad joined the C&O in the development of port facilities at Newport News, Virginia, which gave the Big Four an Atlantic port outlet. Later, this partnership created access to St. Louis, over Big Four tracks, for Chesapeake & Ohio trains from the east.

An amusing commentary on railroad passenger traffic patterns was made in an advertisement of the C&O in 1946. It began by saying that a hog could travel across the country without changing trains, but a human being could not. It mentioned Chicago as "an invisible barrier down the middle of the United States, which you cannot cross without inconvenience, lost time and trouble." It indicated that the situation in St. Louis and New Orleans was comparable.

During the heyday of passenger traffic, the Chesapeake & Ohio Railway adopted the sleeping Chessie Cat as its symbol of comfort aboard such fine trains as the *George Washington,* the *Sportsman* and the *FFV.* In 1971, the C&O operated its last passenger train, before the advent of Amtrak.

In conforming to the trend toward mega-railroad systems, the C&O formed the Chessie System in 1973. In its takeover of the Baltimore & Ohio and the Western Maryland railroads, the Chessie produced a great coal-carrying system reaching from Chesapeake Bay to the Great Lakes and into Canada. Six years later, the Chessie System combined with the Seaboard Coast Line, the Louisville & Nashville and other railroads in the Family Lines to form the CSX Corporation, with 26,600 miles of track. The Chessie System and the CSX in 1979 were not formed by mergers, but were huge common ownerships wherein each component railroad company maintained its separate identity and administration.

# THE ST. LOUIS & SOUTHEASTERN
# AND THE LOUISVILLE & NASHVILLE

Access to St. Louis for the Louisville & Nashville Railroad originated with the St. Louis & Southeastern Railroad, which became its St. Louis Division. The St. Louis & Southeastern was chartered by Illinois in 1869 and, in conjunction with two other lines, created a main line from St. Louis to Evansville, Indiana. In 1880 it became part of the Louisville & Nashville, giving that railroad a much needed connection to St. Louis. In 1882, L&N trains from St. Louis reached Louisville, by agreement with the "Louisville Air Line," which connected with the L&N at Mount Vernon, Illinois. The Louisville Air Line, so-called because of its as-the-crow-flies route, was officially known as the Louisville, Evansville & St. Louis Consolidated Railroad.

The origin of the Louisville & Nashville Railroad is owed to James Guthrie, a prominent Kentucky lawyer who foresaw the commercial advantages of such a route in 1850. Despite much trouble and damage during the Civil War and financial difficulties later, the Louisville & Nashville expanded deeper into the South and became known, with good reason, as "Old Reliable." By 1950 the L&N had 5,250 miles of track and operated the crack passenger train, the *Georgian,* from St. Louis to Atlanta.

A merger of the L&N and the Nashville, Chattanooga & St. Louis Railway occurred in 1959; in 1971 it absorbed the Chicago, Indianapolis & Louisville (Monon Route) and the Memphis branch of the Chicago & Eastern Illinois Railroad. The Louisville & Nashville joined the Seaboard Coast Line in 1975 to form the Family Lines System holding company, which combined with the Chessie System in 1979 to become the CSX Corporation.

# Nashville, Chattanooga & St. Louis Railway

A major component of the Louisville & Nashville after the 1959 merger was the 957-mile Nashville, Chattanooga & St. Louis Railway, which was the first railroad completed in the state of Tennessee. It was originally advocated in 1843 by Dr. James Overton, who visualized it as a railroad project that would permit control of the large cotton trade of Georgia and Alabama.

The first train ran the 11 miles from Nashville to Antioch on April 13, 1851. By May 1853 the line had reached Bridgeport, Alabama, on the Tennessee River and a link with Chattanooga was made by steamboats. The 151-mile line to Chattanooga was opened in February 1854.

A prized relic of the Civil War is the locomotive *General*, which participated in a Union scheme to sever Confederate railroad facilities between Chattanooga and Atlanta on the Western & Atlantic Railroad, later a part of the NC&StL. The *General* led a wild pursuit by Confederates, who despite track and bridge destruction by Union saboteurs, finally caught up with it at Ringgold, Georgia, forcing the culprits to flee into the woods. For many years the *General* was displayed at the NC&StL station in Chattanooga.

Trains of the Nashville, Chattanooga & St. Louis Railway into St. Louis were operated over the tracks of the Louisville & Nashville Railroad from Evansville and Nashville.

Throughout its career, the NC&StL never passed through any form of reorganization, nor ever compromised or failed to pay any obligations.

The *World's Fair Bulletin* of 1901 helps residents of Dixieland and the Delta find their way north to St. Louis.

# THE CAIRO SHORT LINE
# AND THE MOBILE & OHIO

In 1865, the Cairo & St. Louis Railroad Company was chartered in Illinois to construct a narrow-gauge line from East St. Louis to Cairo, and the line was finally opened ten years later. After a reorganization and a name change to St. Louis & Cairo Railroad in 1882, the 196-mile line was popularly called the "Cairo Short Line." In 1886, it was absorbed by the Mobile & Ohio Railroad, which widened its trackage to standard gauge. This enabled the M&O to reach St. Louis as the northern terminus of its route from Mobile, Alabama.

The Mobile & Ohio was organized in 1848 by Mobile interests to tap business from steamboats at Cairo for the faster mode of rail transport to the South. Delayed by the Civil War and its aftermath, the M&O at last reached its destination on the Ohio River in 1883. In 1904, it was called "The Bee Line South" and advertised diners and through sleeping cars from St. Louis to New Orleans. By 1920, the M&O was operating six trains daily into St. Louis Union Station.

In 1940, the Mobile & Ohio merged with the Gulf, Mobile & Northern Railroad, which styled itself "The Rebel Route." Seven years later the GM&O acquired the failing Chicago & Alton Railroad. It then had both Northern and Southern trains, including the *Rebel* and the *Abraham Lincoln.*

In 1972, the Gulf, Mobile & Ohio and the Illinois Central railroads combined to form the Illinois Central Gulf System, with 9,600 miles of track.

# THE SOUTHERN RAILWAY SYSTEM

A comparatively late arrival on the St. Louis railroad scene was the Southern Railway, chartered in Virginia in 1894. Its St. Louis connection was achieved later in the 1890s through its acquisition of the Louisville, Evansville & St. Louis Consolidated Railroad, popularly known as the Louisville Air Line, because of its direct route. It was built in the early 1880s and extended from Louisville to St. Louis, with branches to Evansville, Rockport, and Cannelton. The Southern Railway joined the Terminal Railroad Association of St. Louis in 1902; by 1920 it had six trains using Union Station daily. At that time, the Southern's trains crossed the Mississippi River on Eads Bridge.

While it is possible for the Southern Railway System to trace its lineage back to 1830 and the locomotive *Best Friend of Charleston*, creation of the well-run and profitable system was the result of an evolutionary process of reorganizing southern railroads by John Pierpont Morgan in the latter part of the nineteenth century. He acquired and consolidated more than 20 railroads to form the Southern Railway by 1894.

The Southern enjoyed sustained growth within its territory, especially after World War II. On its eastern lines, the Southern's deluxe trains included the *Crescent* and the *Piedmont Limited*. On the Chicago to Florida run it operated the *Ponce de Leon* and the *Royal Palm*. It truly lived up to its slogan: "The Southern Serves the South."

When Amtrak began in 1971, the Southern was one of three lines to continue its own passenger train service. Finally in 1979, after suffering annual losses, the Southern abandoned the service.

In 1962, the Southern added the Central of Georgia Railway to its system, and in 1982 it coordinated with the Norfolk & Western to form the Norfolk Southern Corporation, an 18,000-mile railroad network operating in 21 states.

# The McKinley Lines and the Illinois Terminal System

An interurban trolley line transformed into a modern railroad—that is the story of the Illinois Terminal System. It had its start in 1890 when William B. McKinley, an electric utility owner and later United States senator from Illinois, purchased the Urbana-Champaign Street Railway Company.

In 1903 he built an interurban line from Danville to Champaign, which soon became known as the Illinois Traction or McKinley System. It was later expanded and extended southward to Granite City. In 1906, Illinois Traction sought entry into St. Louis, and proposed construction of a bridge across the Mississippi River from Venice, Illinois, along with requisite rights-of-way to a downtown terminal in St. Louis. McKinley Bridge was opened in 1910, including a line to a passenger terminal at Twelfth Street and Lucas Avenue.

In the years before automobiles made encroachments on its passenger traffic, Illinois Traction operated day and night three-car electric trains with deluxe equipment between St. Louis and Peoria and Champaign. The *Capitol Limited* ran on a five-hour and 43 minute schedule to Peoria. The *Owl* and the *Illini* night trains, to Peoria and Champaign respectively, featured sleeping cars with windows in their upper berths.

Later, the system assumed the Illinois Terminal Railroad name and in 1932 it occupied a passenger station in the Central Terminal Building at Twelfth and Delmar in St. Louis. It entered this lower level station through a tunnel under Twelfth Boulevard (now Tucker) on a line that also included elevated and surface trackage from McKinley Bridge.

Heavy increases in competition from automobiles and bus lines marked the end of the Illinois Terminal long-distance passenger service. After sleeping cars were taken out of service in 1940, night trains consisted only of coaches. After a revival during World War II due to gasoline rationing, the Illinois Terminal experienced a steady decline in passenger service.

In an unsuccessful effort to stem the tide, ITS ordered three new streamliners, the first of which went into service in November 1948. They cost nearly a million dollars and were the last word in rail travel, with reclining chair cars, luxurious lounge cars, and beautiful diners. Unfortunately, the business was gone.

On March 3, 1953, the St. Louis–Alton commuter trains were replaced by buses; the last long-distance runs were discontinued three years later. Until June 1958 ITS operated a street car service from Granite City to St. Louis, the last remnant of its once extensive electric railway passenger service entering St. Louis. In 1972, the Illinois Terminal had become an all-electric diesel railroad running on 280 miles of its own tracks and an additional 264 miles of trackage rights.

For many years several railroads entering St. Louis had cast covetous eyes upon the ITS with its trackage in St. Louis and the heavily industrialized region across the river. The inevitable happened on July 22, 1981, when the Illinois Terminal Railroad was acquired by the giant Norfolk & Western Railway Company. Interstate Commerce Commission approval was given when it was agreed that the merger would allow consolidation of redundant facilities and operations.

St. Louis Post-Dispatch

**The holiday Midway mobs of the 1950s evaporated in the 1960s, as the nation took to air travel. They would not return again until the Station's renovation in 1985.**

St. Louis Globe-Democrat

"I'll be home for Christmas...if only in my dreams." The poignant WWII song captured the feelings of servicemen who spent the holiday far from home. Local carolers did their best to cheer them up.

# PART III

*Limiteds, Expresses, and Specials*

Shiny new Pullman cars were one of the wonders of the Transportation Pavilion at the 1904 St. Louis World's Fair.

# Leslie's

## *Illustrated Weekly Newspaper*
### *Established in 1855*

Drawn by
*L. Fellows*

AMERICA—THE LAND FOR TOURISTS

## HOW TO SEE AMERICA, BY BURTON HOLMES

# LIMITEDS, EXPRESSES, AND SPECIALS

During its long career as a railroad terminal from 1894 to 1978, St. Louis Union Station witnessed many changes in the trains coming and going from its great trainshed.

Between the 1890s and 1950, the scheduled time from St. Louis to New York was reduced from 28½ to 20 hours. Steam engines, which propelled all trains until the mid-1930s, were gradually supplanted by sleek electro-diesel locomotives for freight and passenger use.

In appearance, passenger cars changed from the effulgently decorated "vestibuled" coaches of the late-Victorian era into streamlined cars with all the modern conveniences. Soon after the turn of the century, wooden passenger coaches were replaced by steel-frame cars. In 1906, the first all-steel passenger cars were placed in service, adding to the safety of train travel.

In 1934 the first successful streamlined lightweight trains were introduced. They were designed to reduce wind resistance, thereby permitting greater speed.

Air-conditioning ("ice actuated") made its appearance on Pullman cars as early as 1929, and by the advent of the streamliners it had become an important element of railroad travel comfort. Long-distance train travel was enhanced by Pullman's innovation of separate roomettes and bedrooms, which afforded greater space than sleeping car berths.

Dining cars, which originated in the late 1860s, improved over the years until their cuisine was comparable to that of the finest restaurants. An important event in railroad history was the introduction of the first all-electric dining car in 1949.

Along with the glamour trains, St. Louis Union Station was host to every celebrity who visited St. Louis during the railroad era—presidents, royalty, political and military leaders, and an impressive list of notables from entertainment, sports, religion, music, art, and all fields of human endeavor.

Some of the passenger trains themselves even became celebrities. Their names were status symbols of the times, and their stories assume a position of major importance in railroad history.

St. Louis Globe-Democrat

**The morning after, 1948: President Harry Truman pauses at Union Station after his reelection to have a laugh on the Chicago newspaper that got it wrong.**

Foldout: Donald Sarno Collection

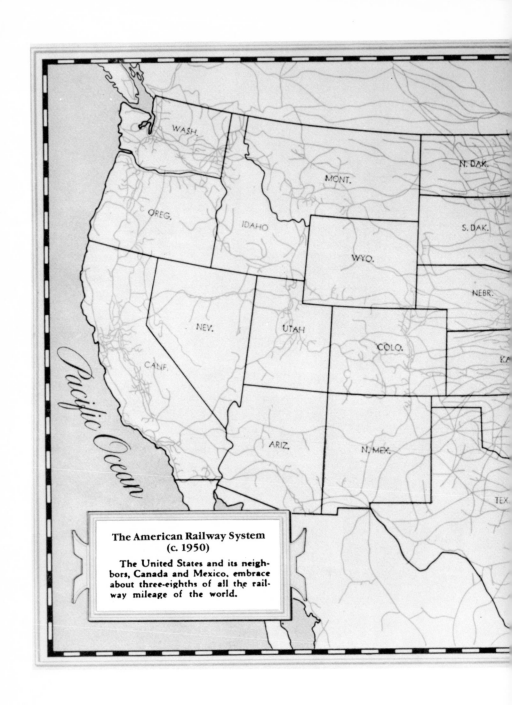

**The American Railway System
(c. 1950)**

The United States and its neighbors, Canada and Mexico, embrace about three-eighths of all the railway mileage of the world.

The *Sunshine Special*, intended for vacationers, became a workhorse during the war, when it carried thousands of soldiers and sailors to Southern army camps and naval bases.

# MISSOURI PACIFIC RAILROAD

Several railroads that had headquarters in St. Louis were prime carriers to the South and Southwest. One of these was the Missouri Pacific, whose flagship train for many years was the famous *Sunshine Special*. From its inception in 1915, the *Sunshine* was recognized as one of America's outstanding trains. By the mid-1920s it was touted for providing service equal to the finest hotels'—luxurious sleeping accommodations, perfect dining car service, and exceptional attention to the comfort and pleasure of its patrons—from St. Louis to San Antonio, California, and Mexico. In 1927 Pullman delivered eight new buffet-lounge-sleeping-observation cars for use on various legs of the *Sunshine Special* routes.

By 1939 that train featured a deluxe observation-lounge car equipped with shower bath, valet, fountain lounge and radio. At that time other Missouri Pacific trains to the Southwest were the *Texan, Southerner, Tennessean,* and *Ozarker.* Service to Denver and California was provided by the *Scenic Limited, Missourian,* and the *Sunflower.* Air-conditioning was added to the *Sunshine Special* in 1940. Eight years later that train was superseded by the streamlined *Texas Eagles.*

Dieselization on the Mo Pac began with the *Missouri River Eagle* in 1940, and in 1942 the diesel-powered *Colorado Eagles* replaced the famous *Scenic Limited*. By Missouri Pacific's centennial in 1951, the *Texas Eagle* carried through sleeping cars from New York and Washington to Texas. The *Colorado Eagle* featured planetarium-dome observation cars between St. Louis and Denver, and living room luxury was advertised aboard the streamlined *Eagles*.

Passenger service on the Mo Pac gradually declined. After 1971, some Amtrak trains used the old Mo Pac tracks to Kansas City and Texas.

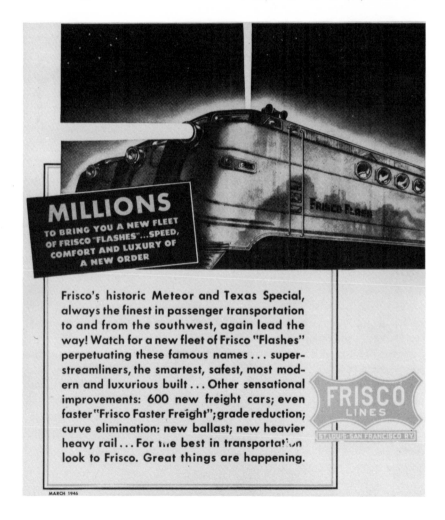

# THE FRISCO AND THE KATY

Two other St. Louis–based railroads, the Frisco and the Katy, joined forces in 1917 to pit the *Texas Special* in competition against Missouri Pacific's *Sunshine Special*. The new train operated over Frisco tracks from St. Louis to Vinita, Oklahoma, and thence on Katy tracks to Dallas–Fort Worth and San Antonio.

Another jointly operated train on these two railroads was the *Bluebonnet* to Texas. In 1947 new dieselized streamline equipment began service on the *Texas Special*, *Bluebonnet*, and Frisco's *Meteor* to Oklahoma. The new cars on the *Texas Special* featured fewer seats per coach, all-room sleepers and a new observation-lounge car, which was described as "really regal." Some other Frisco trains from St. Louis included the *Will Rogers* to Oklahoma, and the *Sunnyland* and the *Memphian* to the South.

On the Katy (the Missouri, Kansas and Texas Lines) another deluxe train from St. Louis to Texas was the famed *Katy Flyer*, a train that dated back to the line's early years. Passenger service on the Frisco and the Katy ended in the 1960s.

# KATY KATY

## M·K·T
### KATY RAILROAD
#### MISSOURI-KANSAS-TEXAS

## M·K·T
### KATY RAILROAD
#### MISSOURI-KANSAS-TEXAS

# TIME TABLES TIME TABLE

CORRECTED TO DECEMBER 1, 1948

FORM 1-135    PRINTED IN U. S. A.

CORRECTED TO DECEMBER 1, 1948

FORM 1-135    PRINTED IN U. S. A.

## THE COTTON BELT ROUTE

Passenger service on the St. Louis–based Cotton Belt Route (St. Louis Southwestern Railway Lines) featured the *Lone Star* and the *Morning Star* trains between St. Louis and Dallas–Fort Worth. The last passenger runs on the Cotton Belt Route were made in December 1959.

*The Modern*
*Ticket Office*

# New Blue Bird On The Wabash

This is the Wabash Railroad's new Budd-built, <u>all</u>-stainless steel Blue Bird, on its winging flight between St. Louis and Chicago. The Blue Bird will make the round trip daily between these two great terminal cities, adding to the completeness of Wabash service and presenting to its passengers comfort and luxury in rail travel previously unknown.

For the Blue Bird is the latest in the roster of distinguished name trains which Budd has created for the modernization of American railroads. Four of its cars are Vista-Domes, giving passengers an unobstructed view of the rolling prairies, picturesque bluffs and river scenery along the way.

Like all Budd-designed, Budd-built equipment, this train illustrates a principle—that better products are made of ideas as well as steel. This was true of the all-steel automobile body which Budd originated and which has made Budd the largest in-

dependent builder of body components in the world. It was true of the steel wheel which Budd developed to take the place of wood. It has been demonstrated in the Budd Disc brake, and in stainless steel highway trailers.

In the railroad field Budd ideas were revolutionary. Ideas that attract passengers by making rail travel more inviting. Ideas that permit faster schedules and yield substantial operating economies. It was Budd vision which led to the whole concept of the modern, stainless steel lightweight streamliner. And Budd today is the only car builder who employs the superior strength of stainless steel to achieve lightweight construction with safety.

The Budd Co., Philadelphia, Detroit

"Follow the Flag"

# THE WABASH

Another railroad that had its head offices in St. Louis for many years was the Wabash, said to be the oldest line in continual service in the Midwest.

Its premier train between St. Louis and Chicago was the *Banner Limited*, so named for the famous Wabash flag trademark. In the 1920s, the route to Chicago became known as the "Rainbow Run" because the principal trains from St. Louis were famed for their colorful exteriors.

The Wabash entry, the *Banner Limited*, was repainted a royal blue with gold striping and was rechristened the *Banner Blue Limited*. It was popularly known as the Blue Train. During the 1940s its time for the run was five and a half hours with steam power. That was later reduced with dieselized and streamlined equipment. Its companion trains to Chicago over the years were the *Midnight Limited* and the *Blue Bird*. By 1950 the latter train became the all-stainless steel *Blue Bird*, which featured Vista Dome cars giving passengers an unobstructed view of the rolling prairies and river scenery along the way. It and the *Banner Blue* soon came to be known as domeliners.

In service between St. Louis and Detroit during the 1930s and 1940s were the daytime *Detroit Special* and the nightly *Detroit Limited*. On the reverse runs they were the *St. Louis Special* and *St. Louis Limited*. An old-line train on this run, the Wabash *Cannonball*, was revived in the 1950s; it ran until the end of operations in 1971.

On the St. Louis–Kansas City run of the Wabash, four trains were operated each way in the 1930s. These were the *Pacific Coast Limited*, *St. Louis–Colorado Limited*, *Kansas City Express*, and the *Midnight Limited*. By 1939 all of the principal trains on the Wabash were air-conditioned.

During the postwar years, the deluxe train on the Kansas City run was the domeliner *City of St. Louis*, which carried through cars to Denver and California. Its running mate was the streamliner *City of Kansas City*. Another Wabash train from St. Louis was the nightly *Omaha Limited*. The *City of St. Louis* was discontinued in 1969 and the *Blue Bird* was terminated in January 1970.

**THE PULLMAN PORTER** obliging and courteous at all times; diligent and cheerful in executing your orders. He assists with your luggage, prepares your berth, and keeps your car, bed and wash-room linen and equipment in orderly fashion. Pullman porters are trained in the art of making you feel at home. They are attentive, but never obtrusive—and they welcome the chance to help you get the most comfort and pleasure out of your trip. On some lines the porter is in charge of the service.

**WHILE THE CONDUCTOR'S** duties are generally associated with receiving passengers, assigning accom-modations, and taking tickets, the most important of his duties at all times and under all conditions is to please and satisfy you. He is interested in your com-fort and welfare and, when you so desire, the porter will be glad to summon him to answer any questions that you may have or wish to ask concerning some particular phase of your trip.

**Fast food, fifties-style: eating on the express. With tablecloths, silverware, and flowers, railroad dining was a gracious occasion.**

# STEAM PASSENGER LOCOMOTIVES

4-4-2 (Atlantic)

4-6-2 (Pacific)

4-6-4 (Hudson)

4-8-2 (Mountain)

4-8-4 (Northern)

## THE ROCK ISLAND

While most of the service on the Rock Island Lines was westward from Chicago, the line operated a coach train from St. Louis to Kansas City during the 1930s. The Missouri Pacific in St. Louis also offered connections with the Rock Island's *Golden State Limited* at Kansas City.

Roy F. Blackburn

**Rock Island motor car no. 9071 on St. Louis—Kansas City train 23.**

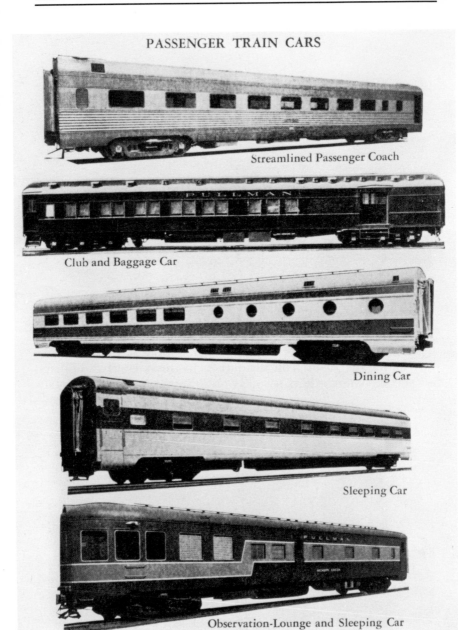

PASSENGER TRAIN CARS

Streamlined Passenger Coach

Club and Baggage Car

Dining Car

Sleeping Car

Observation-Lounge and Sleeping Car

# THE BURLINGTON ROUTE

In 1894 the Burlington Route was a pioneer at the new St. Louis Union Station, when its *Fast Mail* was the first train to depart from the vast trainshed on opening day.

During the steam-power era of railroading, the Burlington operated trains from St. Louis to Kansas City, to Hannibal, Quincy, Burlington, and St. Paul–Minneapolis, as well as to the Twin Cities via Galesburg and Rock Island, Illinois.

After the streamlined Burlington *Zephyr* trains were introduced in 1934, the line operated the *General Pershing Zephyr* and the *Night Hawk* to Kansas City and Denver. Northward from St. Louis, Burlington trains included the *Mark Twain Zephyr* to Hannibal, Missouri, and Burlington, Iowa. In conjunction with the Rock Island Lines, it ran the *Zephyr Rocket* from St. Louis to the Twin Cities, as well as trains through Galesburg, Illinois, northward to the same destination. The *General Pershing* and *Mark Twain Zephyrs* and the *Night Hawk* to Kansas City were jointly operated by the Burlington and the Alton Railroad.

# Nothing Finer on a Diner!

From immaculate kitchens to your table, attentive waiters bear the memorable dishes for which Katy diners are world-famous ... tantalizing delicacies each more satisfying than the last ... topped off with the most wonderful coffee you've ever tasted!

## Famous..

a la carte meals, to suit your purse and pleasure ... table d'hote service providing fine foods at moderate prices ... And, as a special attraction, "Katy Club Meals" at popular prices.

### Sample Menus

**Special Club Breakfast**
**75c**
Choice of
Wheat or Corn Cakes          Cereal
Two Eggs (Boiled, Fried, or Scrambled)
Dry or Buttered Toast
Coffee or Tea (cup), or Milk
(If Fruit Juice is desired, 20c additional)

**Special Club Luncheon**
**$1.05**
Choice of
Turkey Hash or
Macaroni and Ham, au gratin, or
Baked Meat Loaf Creole
with
Potatoes          Fresh Vegetable
Coffee, Tea or Milk
Club Portion, Pie, Ice Cream or Pudding served
with the above Special Club Meal, 25c Extra.

**Special Club Dinner**
**$1.25**
Choice of
Breaded Veal Cutlet, Tomato Sauce or
Chicken a la King on Toast or
Fresh Gulf Fish Fillet
with
Potatoes          Fresh Vegetable
Coffee, Tea or Milk
Club Portion, Pie, Ice Cream or Pudding s
with the above Special Club Meal, 25c I

# CHICAGO & ALTON RAILROAD

A pioneering railroad in Illinois, the Chicago & Alton was the first line to operate through service from St. Louis to Chicago. The wooden-car *Alton Limited* was built by Pullman in 1899, bearing the familiar red color of the line.

In 1924 the all-new *Alton Limited* was introduced by the Chicago & Alton. Brand-new from the front of the locomotive to the observation car platform, the twin limiteds represented an investment of more than a million dollars. There were two complete trains, one with cars named for Illinois and Chicago and its suburbs and the other named for Missouri and St. Louis and its suburbs. Each also included cars named for ex-presidents of the United States. Interiors of the cars were finished in rosewood, while the exteriors were rich maroon with gold striping and silver roofs. With four railroads competing for the St. Louis–Chicago trade, the Alton felt justified in indulging in such an extraordinary luxury with its new limiteds.

By 1940, the Alton advertised 12 trains daily between St. Louis and Chicago, including the *Alton Limited* and the streamliners *Abraham Lincoln* and *Ann Rutledge*, all completely air-conditioned. Another popular train then was the all-Pullman *Midnight Special*. At that time, three trains made the Alton run to Kansas City. These were the *General Pershing Zephyr*, *Mark Twain Zephyr*, and the *Night Hawk*, all operated jointly with the Burlington.

The *Ann Rutledge,* one of the Alton's "personality" trains, crosses the trestle under Eads Bridge as it enters St. Louis.

GM&O Historical Society Archives

**Passengers were welcome to stretch their legs in the lounge car, which featured overstuffed furniture, writing facilities, and a smoking area.**

**Some lounge cars could be adapted for dining.**

# THE ILLINOIS CENTRAL

The St. Louis to Chicago line of the Illinois Central was established in 1899. It inaugurated two deluxe passenger trains the next year. These were the *Diamond Special* and the *Daylight Special*. By the 1920s the *Daylight Special*, painted black and brown below the sill line and a bright green above, was popularly called the Green Train, and by 1947 it was simply the *Daylight*. It went out of service in 1961, leaving the *Green Diamond* as the only Illinois Central train from St. Louis to Chicago. The *Green Diamond*, a pioneer diesel-electric streamliner, had been put into service in May 1936 after a system-wide tour.

The *Night Diamond*, begun as the *Diamond Special* in 1900, was one of the first trains to use Pullman's all-bedroom cars, along with the *Panama Limited*, in 1930. In the 1940s the *Night Diamond* was the Illinois Central's entry in a three-way competition with the Wabash and the Alton, all of which had trains leaving St. Louis Union Station a few minutes before midnight bound for Chicago.

For many years, trains from St. Louis also connected with the IC main line at Carbondale, Illinois, joining trains from Chicago to New Orleans and Florida.

# CHICAGO & EASTERN ILLINOIS

Achieving its entry into St. Louis in time for the 1904 World's Fair, the Chicago & Eastern Illinois Railroad was the fourth line furnishing St. Louis–Chicago service. An early train on that line was the *St. Louis Zipper*, which had a flat five-hour schedule to Chicago.

During Chicago's World's Fair, the Century of Progress Exposition in 1933-1934, the C&E operated two air-conditioned trains from St. Louis to Chicago. These were the fast daylight train the *Century of Progress* and the popular night train the *Spirit of Progress*. They featured cafe-lounge cars with radio and valet service.

In 1947 the line's trains on the Chicago run were the *Zipper* and a night train called the *Silent Knight*.

**This striking suspension building housed the Travel and Transportation exhibit at the 1933 Chicago World's Fair. Although the trains it displayed remained popular for years, this architectural style never caught on.**

**After World War II, the Baltimore and Ohio made special arrangements with Mo Pac to serve the South.**

# BALTIMORE & OHIO RAILROAD

St. Louis attained through railroad service to Washington, D.C., and Baltimore with the creation of the Baltimore & Ohio Southwestern Railroad in 1893. Later, service was extended to Jersey City and New York via the Reading Railway Lines and the Central Railroad of New Jersey.

The premier train from St. Louis on the Baltimore & Ohio was the *National Limited*, which began service in 1925. It achieved an on-time record of 98 percent on its 882-mile run between St. Louis and Washington. Although it was discontinued after the B&O affiliated with the Chesapeake & Ohio, the name *National Limited* was used later on an Amtrak train from Kansas City through St. Louis to New York until 1979.

In 1947, the B&O operated the *National Limited* and the *Diplomat* as diesel-electric feature trains from St. Louis to Washington and New York. Other trains on that run were the *Metropolitan Special* and the New York *Night Express*. The B&O also ran trains from St. Louis to Louisville. After World War II, arrangements with the Frisco, Katy, and Missouri Pacific enabled the B&O to provide through service to Texas and Oklahoma.

# NEW YORK CENTRAL'S
## *NEW Luxury Coaches—*
### adding enchantment to your first post-war vacation!

FIVE solid gleaming miles of luxury coaches are rolling off the production lines. They're alive with the up-to-the-minute features for which thousands of New York Central passengers voted. And many of these cars of tomorrow are ready today for your first post-war vacation. Ready to carry you, at low coach fares, on your way to the Adirondacks, New England, Niagara Falls, Canada, the Great Lakes or the Western Wonderlands.

### *Vacation all the Way!*

Your vacation starts the minute you board one of these smooth-riding streamlined coaches...with their advanced air conditioning and extra wide sightseeing windows.

### *Best dressed Dressing Rooms!*

Smart, spacious dressing lounges feature streamlined fixtures, lighted mirrors, electric outlets for curling iron or razor . . . the latest appointments for your comfort.

### *Try this for Size!*

Lots of leg room in the new feather-soft seats. Touch a plastic knob and they adjust instantly for reading or resting. *And*...on many trains, your seat is reserved at no extra charge.

*Coming—* **CARS ENOUGH FOR 52 NEW STREAMLINERS TO UNDERLINE THE *NEW* IN *NEW YORK CENTRAL!***

## NEW YORK CENTRAL

*The Scenic Water Level Route*

NEW YORK CENTRAL SYSTEM

# NEW YORK CENTRAL SYSTEM

As a St. Louis version of the *Twentieth Century Limited*, the *Southwestern Limited* was introduced by the New York Central–Big Four with all new Pullman equipment in 1904. It was the Central's flagship St. Louis train for more than 50 years. After World War II, the *Southwestern* made its debut as a stainless steel streamlined dieseliner. Its Pullman cars contained all private bedrooms for passengers' sleeping comfort. Circulating ice water and individually controlled air-conditioning were among the new conveniences. Increased space in all cars was a hallmark of the *Southwestern Limited*, as it was of the *Twentieth Century*.

Other fine New York Central dieseliners from St. Louis were the *Knickerbocker* and the *Missourian*. At St. Louis Union Station, convenient platform-to-platform connections to the West and Southwest were made easily from these trains. New York Central trains to Cleveland and Buffalo included the *Cleveland–St. Louis Special* and the *Gateway*.

THE
AMERICAN

# PENNSYLVANIA RAILROAD

When St. Louis Union Station opened in 1894, the Vandalia-Pennsylvania Railroad was operating four trains daily between St. Louis and New York.

Among the Pennsylvania Railroad's best trains on its St. Louis to New York run from 1908 to 1927 were the eastbound *New Yorker* and the westbound *St. Louisan*. In 1927 they were rechristened the *Spirit of St. Louis* in commemoration of Charles A. Lindbergh's transatlantic flight in that famous plane.

A few years before, the Pennsy had inaugurated its finest St. Louis to New York train, the extra-fast and extra-fare *American*, designed to rival the famed *Broadway Limited*. It was said to be as "fully equipped for comfort as a perfectly appointed town club, as well as creating the delightful informality of your home." Passengers were assured they would feel the luxury the moment they boarded this "outstanding institution of deluxe transportation." Conveniences available included an office secretary-stenographer, barber, valet, and telephone service from the train at its terminals. Books, magazines, and newspapers were provided in the *American*'s lounge-observation car. Women patrons had maids and a manicurist at their disposal. Dining on the *American* was described as an epicurean masterpiece.

In later years the all-Pullman *American* had a deluxe all-coach running mate, the *Jeffersonian*. In that train's post-World War II version, coach seating accommodated 44 passengers instead of the former 56, allowing more legroom for passengers in the deeply upholstered reclining lounge chairs. Six-foot-wide windows of shatterproof glass, glareless lighting, air-conditioning and pastel wall colors were featured in these deluxe coaches.

Some other popular Pennsy trains to New York from St. Louis during the 1920s and 1930s were the *Keystone Express*, *Commercial Express*, *Juniata*, *Gotham Limited*, and *Mercantile Express*. In the late 1930s some favorite trains from St. Louis were the *Pennsylvania Limited* and the *Metropolitan*, a revived version of the *St. Louisan* and the *Liberty Limited* to Washington. New trains added during the 1940s included the *Golden Arrow* and the *Duquesne* to Pittsburgh.

By 1947, a daily through train traveled on the Pennsylvania line to St. Louis and thence to several Texas cities on the Missouri Pacific and Texas Pacific. It operated as the *Sunshine Special* on all three lines. By 1963 this train had become the *Penn-Texas*. Through cars on the *American* in 1947 provided service to Oklahoma via the Frisco and the Katy.

With the decline in railroad passenger traffic by 1963, the Pennsy's St. Louis to New York fleet consisted of the streamliners *Penn-Texas*, the *St. Louisan*, and the *Spirit of St. Louis*. The latter was the sole survivor on the Penn-Central in March 1971.

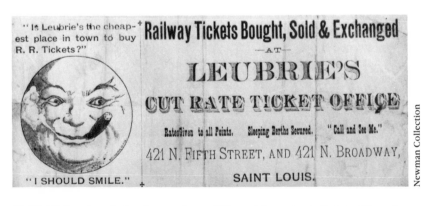

**Getting it for you wholesale was the ambition of the cut-rate ticket offices that proliferated near Union Station.**

**Strangers on a train found a chance to become better acquainted in the observation car.**

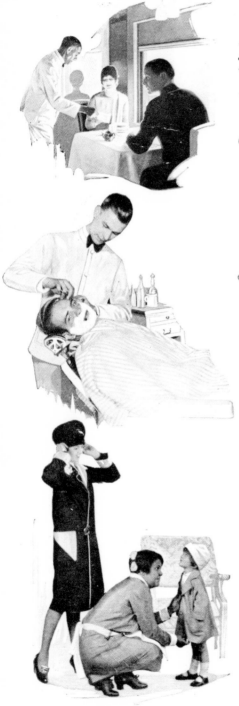

# Food
## *for*
# Epicures

*Not one thing need be
omitted from your daily
life's round. A skillful
barber is ready to give
you the trim or shave you
failed to get in your rush
for the train.*

*Women and children
have not been forgotten on
this perfectly appointed
train. An experienced
maid for them is waiting
to be called to perform
any personal service
needed.*

# THE NICKEL PLATE ROAD

After securing direct entry into St. Louis in 1923, the Nickel Plate Road began daily service from St. Louis to Cleveland, where connections could be made for New York.

In 1950, Pullman-Standard redesigned all-room sleepers for the Nickel Plate. The car "City of Lorain" had a stainless-steel exterior with extra-wide windows and a blue letterboard. The higher-priced double-bed rooms were located in the smoother-riding center of the car.

The Nickel Plate, officially known as the New York, Chicago and St. Louis Railroad, also operated trains to Toledo and Detroit and connected with the Delaware, Lackawanna & Western Railroad at Buffalo for service to New York.

**Extra-fare luxury trains offered the amenities of first-class hotels: maids, barbers, secretaries and special cuisine.**

# You feel the lingering presence of a gracious past

On trains as modern as their air-conditioning, you find a hospitable spirit that already was tradition when George Washington was a youth. Born in the charming inns of the old South, it lives again in the *Tavern Cars* of Chesapeake and Ohio Lines ... You meet it in many delightful forms —in the courtesy cup of coffee and the newspaper placed before you at breakfast ... reflected in the tasteful furnishings ... in the cheerful solicitude of steward and waiters ... perfectly expressed in southern-style cooking and serving of delicious foods at friendly low prices ... Yes, in these modern Tavern Cars is recaptured an atmosphere in which gracious ladies in crinoline would feel pleasantly at home.

## IMAGINE THIS DINNER FOR ONLY 75¢

THE TAVERN DINNER offers you first a tempting appetizer, then choice of fish, meats or fowl in traditional Virginia styles...accompanied by fresh vegetables, a salad and assorted breads ... topped off by choice of desserts and beverages.

Also served at moderate cost are a variety of breakfast combinations and the luxurious Mount Vernon Dinner.

For information and aid in planning trips, write Chesapeake and Ohio Travel Se 827 E. Main St., Richmond, Va.

*Sleep like a Kitten*

## THE CHESSIE CORRIDOR

*The Scenic Route of the East*

George Washington's Railroad
CHESAPEAKE and OHI
*Lines*
Original Predecessor Company Founded by George Washington in 17

® *"Sleep Like a Kitten"*

# CHESAPEAKE AND OHIO RAILWAY

Long known as "George Washington's Railroad," the Chesapeake & Ohio marked the bicentennial anniversary of Washington's birth with the introduction of its flagship glamour train the *George Washington*, on April 24, 1932.

It was advertised as the "Most Wonderful Train in the World." Each of its cars bore a name related to some aspect of Washington's part in American history. They were decorated in colonial style. In 1950 the *George Washington* was reintroduced as a streamlined dieseliner. The train was so popular that it carried more than 15 million passengers in its first 25 years of service. In a "step to merger" approved by the Interstate Commerce Commission, the Chesapeake & Ohio became jointly operated with the Baltimore & Ohio, but some cars of the *George Washington* still ran into St. Louis Union Station. In 1947 it carried through cars from Washington to San Antonio via the Missouri Pacific. Other C&O cars came to St. Louis over New York Central tracks from Cincinnati on the *Sportsman*.

**Railroad china may have reached its apogee on the Chessie's *George Washington*, which used a Stuart portrait of Washington on its gold-rimmed service plates.**

Richard Luckin Collection:
*Dining on Rails*

 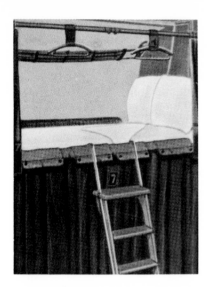

*Top:* **Although it wasn't spacious, the upper berth had an electric light, a shelf, hangers, and a button to summon the helpful porter.**

*Bottom:* **The lower berth offered these conveniences and one more—the right to sit in the forward-facing seat during the daytime.**

# LOUISVILLE & NASHVILLE RAILROAD

A direct connection between St. Louis and the South began in 1880 when the Louisville & Nashville Railroad acquired the St. Louis & Southeastern line to Evansville, Indiana.

In 1947 a new all-coach streamliner with reserved seats at no extra charge, the *Georgian*, was operated by the L&N between St. Louis and Atlanta using L&N trackage as far as Nashville. It featured comfortable, adjustable seats, wide-vision windows, air conditioning, train attendants, and a public address system in every car. Fine Southern cuisine was served in smart diners at popular prices. Tavern lounge cars provided relaxation for reading, enjoying refreshments, or listening to favorite radio programs. The *Georgian* ran on a fast 12-hour-52-minute schedule between its terminals. In 1953 the L&N purchased new standardized all-room sleeping cars from Pullman for the use on the *Georgian*.

Two trains from St. Louis and Chicago to Florida that operated every third day in the winter of 1947 were the *Dixieland* and the *Florida Arrow*. Running daily at that time from St. Louis to Florida, via Nashville, were the L&N *Dixie Flyer* and the *Dixie Limited*. Three trains each way between St. Louis and New Orleans, via Mobile, were operated by L&N in 1947, as well as several trains to Louisville and Nashville.

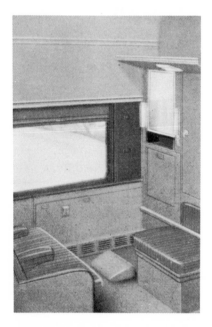

*Top:* The double bedroom gave passengers extra elbow room. It sported its own toilet, mirror, air-conditioning, and even a thermos bottle.

*Bottom:* The roomette's features included a special compartment for the passenger's shoes—so the porter could discreetly remove them, shine them, and return them.

## NASHVILLE, CHATTANOOGA & ST. LOUIS RAILROAD ("THE DIXIE LINE")

In the 1940s sections of the *Dixie Limited* and the *Dixie Flyer* were operated daily from St. Louis Union Station over L&N tracks to Nashville and thence to Atlanta on the Nashville, Chattanooga & St. Louis Railroad. Service to Florida from Atlanta was offered on trackage of other southern railroads. The NC&StL, whose predecessor lines dated from before the Civil War, merged with the Louisville & Nashville Railroad in 1959.

**Go RAIL AND Pullman**

PULLMAN

THE COMFORTABLE AND SURE WAY TO GET THERE
. . . WITH ALL THE SPEED THAT'S SAFE!

# GULF, MOBILE & OHIO RAILROAD

After widening its trackage to standard gauge by 1886, the Mobile & Ohio Railroad reached St. Louis. By the turn of the century, its direct route from St. Louis Union Station to New Orleans caused the M&O to be called the "Bee-Line South."

In 1940 the Mobile & Ohio merged with its long-time rival the Gulf, Mobile & Northern Railroad, also known as the "Rebel Route." The new railroad, called the Gulf, Mobile & Ohio, by 1946 was operating the *Gulf Coast Rebel* from St. Louis to Mobile and Montgomery, Alabama, and the *Rebel* between St. Louis and New Orleans.

That same year, the GM&O acquired the Chicago & Alton Railroad in a merger. As a result, the line presented a geographical contrast, running the *Rebel* trains in the South and trains named *Abraham Lincoln* and *Ann Rutledge* in the North, on the tracks of the former Alton Railroad.

The pride of the Gulf, Mobile & Ohio was the silver and crimson diesel-electric streamlined *Gulf Coast Rebel*, whose consist included all-room Pullmans and luxury coaches.

# SOUTHERN

## RAILWAY SYSTEM

### PASSENGER TRAIN SCHEDULES

# SOUTHER

## RAILWAY SYSTEM

### PASSENGER TRAIN SCHEDULES

APRIL 30, 1961

APRIL 30, 1961

# SOUTHERN RAILWAY SYSTEM

The Southern Railway System was chartered in 1894, the same year that St. Louis Union Station opened. The Southern achieved its St. Louis connection later through acquisition of the so-called Louisville Air Line, famous for its direct route.

The Southern's territory experienced continual growth, making good its boast "The Southern Serves the South." On its rail link between St. Louis Union Station and Louisville, the Southern ran connecting trains to join with such main line trains as the *Ponce De Leon*, the *Royal Palm* and the *Carolina Special*. The first two went to Florida and the latter to Greensboro, North Carolina.

With the coming of Amtrak in 1971, the Southern was one of three railroads desiring to continue its passenger train service. After considerable financial losses, the Southern abandoned that service in 1979, ending an illustrious history of private passenger train operations both for the Southern and for the nation.

**Panorama from top of trainshed looking south, 1949.**

**The Midway from 18th Street, c. 1895.**

# POSTLUDE

Thus we come to the end of the story of the many railroads that provided passenger service to St. Louis for more than a century.

May the memory forever endure of those great railroads and their famous luxury trains: the *American, Jeffersonian,* and *Spirit of St. Louis*; the *National* and *Southwestern Limiteds* and the *George Washington*; the *Sunshine Special,* the *Texan,* and the *Eagles*; the *Bluebonnet, Texas Special, Meteor,* and *Katy Flyer*; the *Banner Blue Limited* and the *City of St. Louis*; the *Abraham Lincoln* and *Ann Rutledge;* the *Alton Limited* and the *Rebel;* the *Green Diamond* and the *Morning Star*; the *Georgian* and the *Dixie Flyer*; the *Sportsman* and the *St. Louisan.* All of these and more called St. Louis Union Station home.

# MEMORIES
*of Union Station*

**St. Louis Union Station touched the lives of hundreds of thousands of people. Although the trains are gone, Union Station lives on in their scrapbooks and memories.**

In the good old days, ragtime music kept the neighborhood humming...

Folks made their way to Union Station
by foot, by carriage, by train, and by trolley.

Everyone who was anyone passed through Union Station...
sooner or later.

**DONT GET LEFT**
**THE KATY FLYER**
**A NEW FAST TRAIN**
VIA

THE
**MK and T**
MISSOURI, KANSAS & TEXAS RAILWAY COMPANY.

LEAVES
UNION STATION **ST. LOUIS**
DAILY AND AT **8.20 P.M.**
SUNDAYS TOO
FOR SEDALIA, NEVADA, FT. SCOTT,
PARSONS, INDIAN TER., DALLAS,
FT. WORTH, WACO, HOUSTON,
SAN ANTONIO and INTERMEDIATE POINTS.

*If you kept your eyes open ... you could spot some familiar faces in the crowd.*

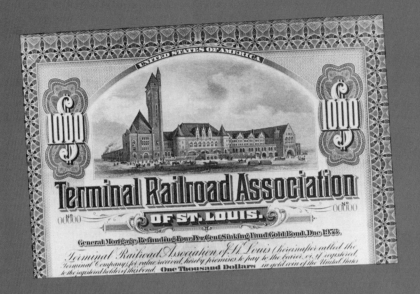

Union Station's size could be overwhelming...
One rustic visitor supposedly spent his whole trip
to St. Louis inside it and was ridiculed when he
told hometown friends that the city had a roof.

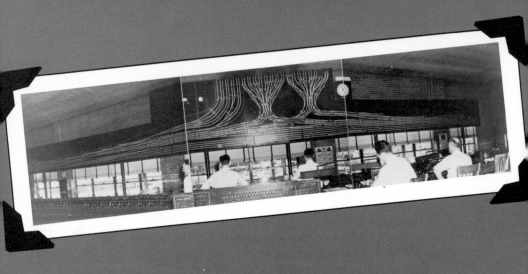

In the 1970s, Union Station got the disappearing
railroad blues ... only the memories remained.

*Credits for Memories section:* pp. 162-163: nickelodeon and Portland Hotel, *St. Louis Globe-Democrat;* handbill, Newman Collection; sheet music, Trebor Tichenor; pp. 164-165: viaduct, Newman Collection; streetcar, Harry Hagen Collection; pp. 166-167: street corner, *Globe-Democrat;* Roosevelt, Otto Saab Collection; Reagan, Missouri Pacific System; pp. 168-169: bond dated 1903, Newman Collection; saloon, Raymond M. Molner Collection; staircase, *Globe-Democrat;* benches, *St. Louis Post-Dispatch;* pp. 170-171: Perry Tower map of system, Donald A. Sarno Collection; trainman, Wayne Leeman Collection.

# BIBLIOGRAPHY

Alexander, Edwin P. *The Pennsylvania Railroad, a Pictorial History.* New York: W. W. Norton Inc., 1947.

———. Down at the Depot. New York: Bramhall House, 1970.

Belcher, Wyatt Winton. *The Economic Rivalry Between St. Louis and Chicago—1850-1880.* New York: Columbia University Press, 1947.

Bernard, William C. *City of St. Louis Railroad Atlas.* St. Louis: Board of Public Service, 1936.

Burlington Northern Railroad. *Predecessors—The Frisco: a Battler and a Survivor.* Chicago: B/N Railroad, 1980.

City Plan Association. *City Plan Report.* St. Louis: 1911.

City Plan Commission. *Problems of St. Louis.* St. Louis: Nixon-Jones Printing Co., 1917.

Civic League of St. Louis. *A City Plan for St. Louis.* St. Louis: 1907.

Clarke, Thomas Curtis, et al. *The American Railway.* New York: Charles Scribner & Sons, 1889.

Compton, Richard J., and Dry, Camille N. *Pictorial St. Louis—1875.* St. Louis: Compton Lithographing Co., 1875.

Conklin, Will. *St. Louis Illustrated.* St. Louis: Will Conklin, 1876.

Corliss, Carlton J. *The Main Line of Mid America—the Story of the Illinois Central.* New York: Creative Age Press, 1950.

Cox, James. *Old and New St. Louis.* St. Louis: Continental Printing Co., 1894.

Droege, John A. *Passenger Terminals and Trains.* New York: McGraw-Hill Book Co., 1916.

Edwards, Richard, and Hopewell, Mena. *The Great West and Her Commercial Metropolis.* St. Louis: 1860.

Fitzsimmons. Bernard. *150 Years of North American Railroads.* Hadley Woods, Herts., England: Winchmore Publishing Services, Ltd., 1982.

Flint, Timothy, *A Condensed Geography and History of the Western States of the Mississippi Valley.* Cincinnati: 1828.

Grow, Lawrence. *Waiting for the 5:05—Terminal, Station and Depot in America.* New York: Main Street/Universe Books, 1977.

Herr, Kincaid A. *The Louisville & Nashville Railroad—1850–1963.* Louisville: L&N Magazine, 1964.

Hogan, Tim. *Railroads Have Helped Move Settlers and Supplies Westward.* St. Louis: St. Louis Globe-Democrat, November 25, 1976.

Holbrook, Stuart H. *The Story of American Railroads.* New York: American Legacy Press, 1947.

Hollingsworth, J. Brian. *The History of American Railroads.* New York: Exeter Books, 1982.

Hungerford, Edward. *The History of the Baltimore & Ohio Railroad.* New York: G. Putnam's Sons, 1928.

———. *Men and Iron—the History of the New York Central.* New York: Thomas Y. Crowell, 1938.

Hyde, William, and Conard, Howard. *Encyclopedia of the History of St. Louis.* St. Louis: Southern History Company, 1899.

Jensen, Oliver. *The American Heritage History of Railroads in America.* New York: American Heritage Publishing Company/Bonanza Books, 1981.

Leeman, Wayne. *City's Last Commuter Train Succumbs to Changing Times.* St. Louis: St. Louis Post-Dispatch, December 10, 1961.

———. *Still Number Two in Rails.* St. Louis: St. Louis Commerce Magazine, October 1977.

Lemly, James Hutton. *The Gulf, Mobile & Ohio—a Railroad That Had To Expand or Expire.* Homewood, Ill.: R. D. Irwin, 1953.

Masterson, V. V. *The Katy Railroad and the Last Frontier.* Norman, Okla.: University of Oklahoma Press, 1952.

Meeks, Carroll. *The Railroad Station.* New Haven, Conn.: Yale University Press, 1960.

Miner, H. Craig. *The St. Louis–San Francisco Transcontinental Railroad.* Lawrence, Kans.: University of Kansas Press, 1972.

Missouri Pacific Railroad. *The First Hundred Years—Missouri Pacific Lines Magazine.* St. Louis: July 1951.

———. *The First 125 Years.* St. Louis: 1976.

———. *Inside Mo Pac.* St. Louis: 1980.

National Railway Publishing Co. *The Official Guide of the Railways.* New York: February 1947.

National Resources Committee. *Regional Planning, Part II—St. Louis Region.* Washington, D.C.: U.S. Government Printing Office, 1936.

Overton, R. C. *The First Ninety Years—1850–1940.* Chicago: Chicago, Burlington & Quincy Railroad, 1940.

Pangborn, J. G. *The World's Railway.* New York: Winchell Printing Company, 1894.

Reavis, Logan U. *St. Louis, the Future Great City of the World.* St. Louis: Grey and Beyer Co., 1876.

Riegel, Robert E. *The Missouri Pacific Railroad to 1879.* Columbia, Mo.: Missouri Historical Review, State Historical Society of Missouri, October 1923.

———. *America Moves West.* New York: Henry Holt & Co., 1946.

St. Louis Chamber of Commerce. *St. Louis As It Is Today.* St. Louis: 1950.

St. Louis Post-Dispatch. *Rock Island: End of a Mighty Good Road.* St. Louis: May 29, 1980.

Scharf, J. Thomas. *History of St. Louis City and County.* Philadelphia: Louis H. Everts Co., 1883.

Schnell, J. Christopher. *Chicago versus St. Louis—a Reassessment of the Great Rivalry.* Columbia, Mo.: Missouri Historical Review, State Historical Society of Missouri, April 1977.

Skinner, Lemoine, Jr., and Messick, Morris. *The Half Page—Wabash, the Main Line to Progress.* St. Louis: St. Louis Post-Dispatch, 1951.

———. *The Half Page—Cotton Belt, a Railroad with an Accent on Fast Freight.* St. Louis: St. Louis Post-Dispatch, 1952.

Smith, C. J., & Co. *Report of Engineer's Committee—St. Louis–East St. Louis Terminals.* St. Louis: 1922.

Stevens, Walter B. *St. Louis—the Fourth City.* St. Louis: S. J. Clarke Publishing Co., 1909.

Terminal Railroad Association of St. Louis. *The St. Louis Union Station, a Monograph.* St. Louis: 1895.

———. *50 Years of Transportation—1894–1944, Union Station and St. Louis.* St. Louis: 1944.

Vandalia-Pennsylvania Railroad. *St. Louis Union Station.* St. Louis: 1895.

Wandell, Harry B. *The Story of a Great City in a Nut Shell.* St. Louis: 1900.

Waring, George E. *Report on the Social Statistics of Cities—Tenth Census of the United States—1880.* Washington, D.C.: U.S. Government Printing Office, 1887.

Wayman, Norbury L. *Life On The River.* New York: Crown Publishers. 1971.

———. *History of St. Louis Neighborhoods Series.* St. Louis: Community Development Agency, 1980.

———. *How St. Louis Grew—the History of Its Appearance.* St. Louis: Community Development Agency, 1981.

### ABOUT THE AUTHOR:

Norbury L. Wayman has spent a lifetime recording the history of St. Louis and the Midwest. He is noted as a local historian, artist, and city planner. His interest in transportation has led to this book about *St. Louis Union Station and Its Railroads*. He is also the author of *Life On the River—A Pictorial History of the Mississippi River System* (Crown Publishers, N.Y., 1971), *A Pictorial History of St. Louis* (1968), *History of the Physical Growth of St. Louis* (1969), and the *History of St. Louis Neighborhoods* series (1980). Sets of his historical maps of St. Louis are in the Library of Congress and the St. Louis Public Library. He is listed in *Who's Who in the Midwest* and is a member of the Landmarks Association of St. Louis, the Missouri Historical Society, the State Historical Society of Missouri, and the National Trust for Historical Preservation.